NORTH NOTTINGHAMSHIRE CHURCH WALKS

Alan & Janet Nash

Published by Sigma Leisure – an imprint of
Sigma Press, 1 South Oak Lane, Wilmslow, Cheshire SK9 6AR, England.

British Library Cataloguing in Publication Data
A CIP record for this book is available from the British Library.

ISBN: 1 85058 777 9

Typesetting and Design by: Sigma Press, Wilmslow, Cheshire.

Cover photograph: St Peter's, East Drayton *(see Walk 14)*

Photographs and Maps: Alan & Janet Nash

Printed by: MFP Design and Print

Disclaimer: the information in this book is given in good faith and is believed to be correct at the time of publication. No responsibility is accepted by either the author or publisher for errors or omissions, or for any loss or injury howsoever caused. Only you can judge your own fitness, competence and experience.

Contents

**Locations of churches
– see Index for walks using these churches**

Introduction

England is blessed with a multitude of magnificent church buildings which dot the landscape, providing walkers with a landmark that can often be seen at great distances and which mark the hub of a village community set deep in the countryside. The problem with writing a walking book based on the churches of north Nottinghamshire is knowing when to stop, for this is such attractive and largely undiscovered country that once you set out, your boots just keep you marching southward. In our case, southerly progress was only halted when the potential size of the publication dictated that we call a halt.

The Walks

For the purpose of this book, we have taken north Nottinghamshire to include the whole of Bassetlaw and the northern part of Newark and Sherwood District, stretching southwards to a point just north of a line running from Newark to Mansfield. Here we have the wide valley of the River Trent constantly to the east while, in the centre and west, the ground rises gently from the northern flatlands, through the Wheatley Hills then continues southward to the magnificent forests of Sherwood. Crossed by the River Idle and the Chesterfield Canal and dotted with tiny villages and beautiful churches, our original intention had been to cover just Bassetlaw and to form walks from every church in that District. Unfortunately, a number of churches just do not lend themselves easily to a circular walk although Beckingham, Low Marnham, Bole and Saundby might have been included — but to have done so would have made the walks either too long or would have necessitated crossing fields frequently grazed by lively livestock. Sadly, Misson, Darlton, Gamston, Sutton cum Lound, Harworth, West Drayton and Littleborough did not fit easily into our scheme and thus the geographical area covered was extended southwards with brief excursions into neighbouring Derbyshire and Yorkshire.

The whole area is well covered by long-distance footpaths and we have frequently made use of these. The ones we shall meet include: the Trent Valley Way, an 84-mile route designed to celebrate the 100th anniversary of the founding of Nottingham County Council; the Cuckoo Way, which follows the banks of the Chesterfield Canal; the Robin Hood Way, which meanders its wonderful way for about 105 miles between Nottingham and Edwinstowe and, finally, the Archaeological Way, which although chiefly within Derbyshire, will be met briefly in Walk 29.

The walks described vary in length from 5 to 11 miles and are designed specifically for the ease of the route. As a very rough guide, a walking speed of between 2 and 2½ miles an hour might be considered plus say, half an hour for each church and, of course, time for drink/lunch stops – this will mean that even the shortest walk should make a pleasant half-day venture. The purist may not be entirely happy with some of the routes we have chosen. In many cases, we have neglected obvious cross-field link paths in favour of country roads and green lanes. However, having spent many years trudging through heavy mud and fighting off bellicose bullocks, we feel that there is little pleasure to be gained from this when there is a perfectly acceptable alternative that allows walking at any time of the year and permits easy progress.

We start and end our walks at Worksop, which is not only the district 'capital' of Bassetlaw but is also 'the gateway to the Dukeries' — the name used to describe that area of Nottinghamshire which formerly contained the estates of the Dukes of Portland, Newcastle, Kingston, Leeds and Norfolk. From here, we move in a clockwise direction around Bassetlaw (and edging into Yorkshire) before dropping down into the northern part of Newark and Sherwood District and moving westwards and northwards back to Worksop (by means of a short excursion into Derbyshire). Although the descriptions were accurate at the time of writing, bear in mind that things do change in the countryside. Waymarkers and finger-posts get damaged and sometimes vegetation might make them difficult to see. Hedges are sometimes removed and new plantations are sometimes planted. Gates may be removed or inserted and stiles might be removed and replaced by gateways. Then again, villages grow and even the names of pubs and inns change. So, please try to keep to the directions given, even though some of the landmarks might not be quite as described.

Above all, please take the relevant Ordnance Survey map with you. This will not only help you follow the route, but will give added interest by showing the countryside around you and relating to other walks described in the area. Start points are, for the most part obvious but we have also given grid references; if you are unsure of how to read these then details are to be found in the margins of the Ordnance Survey map. Where we have used the terms 'diagonally left', 'diagonally right', 'forward' etc, these are the directions to be taken from the line of the obstacle or feature (stile, gate, gap) described. Finally, a headland path is one which runs along the edge of a field, an external field corner is one which protrudes towards you, and an internal field corner is one into which you walk.

The Churches

During the walks we visit a total of 74 churches, two of them (Bothamsall and Laxton) appearing in two walks since the villages themselves are at the centre of such excellent walking areas. Two of the buildings can be classed as 'romantic ruins' and we also call in at a magnificent abbey. The notes about the churches have, for the most part, been kept very brief and, although none of the churches visited could be classed as 'missable', the detail given for some will make it obvious that these were our true favourites and were even more 'unmissable' than others – you may have different views! Unfortunately, it is a fact of life these days that many of the buildings will be locked when you arrive but there will usually be details of where to obtain the key. If you are lucky, you may arrive during a service, or when the church is being decorated for Christmas or Harvest Festival or perhaps when a group of local people are giving their time to clean or tidy the building and then there will be a cheery welcome and a guide will usually be found to conduct you around.

The various developments in church architecture have been divided into 'periods' or 'styles' that are 'typical' of a certain time. Unfortunately, it is impossible to date these periods exactly since the developments would have overlapped and would have arrived in one area earlier or later than in another. Thus, the dates given below must be treated as the very roughest of guides. Another factor is that our forefathers (and ourselves) have had a constant urge to 'improve' the original. Thus to find a church which can be dated to a single period or style is very difficult indeed. It is perhaps this that makes our churches so interesting since a little investigation will quickly uncover 'improvements' made to some buildings covering a period of hundreds of years.

The earliest church building of pre-Norman times was probably little more than a rectangular box sometimes with a special section added to accommodate the priest and altar. We have no buildings dating from this time in north Nottinghamshire but the churches at Cottam and Carburton have the simple box plan, while those at Stokeham and Holbeck (which is a Victorian copy) have the added sanctuary or chancel. We do, though, have some fine masonry of this period including the lower stages of the tower at South Carlton, some stonework at West Markham and the magnificent tympanum at Everton.

The **Norman period** (11th and 12th centuries) saw a significant advance in church building, with the introduction of permanent stone monuments with huge cylindrical pillars and massive rounded arches, many of them carved. We have plenty of examples of Norman work in our area including the internal north aisle at Blyth, at Carburton (although heavily disguised), at Church Warsop, Cottam, Edwinstowe, the north arcades at South Collingham and South Scarle, the chancel arches at Everton and South Wheatley, at West Markham and at Worksop Priory. Some of our towers also show good

Norman work, particularly the lower stages at Church Laneham, Clayworth, Everton, Fledborough and South Leverton but perhaps the most remarkable are examples of Norman doorways to be seen at Church Laneham, Cuckney and South Carlton.

At the end of the 12th century, we have a short period called the **Transitional** (with examples at Church Laneham, Edwinstowe, West Markham and Worksop Priory). Here we see the introduction of the pointed arch and of a little decoration on the pillars which developed into the Gothic period – usually broken down into Early English, Decorated and Perpendicular periods.

The **Early English** style of the 13th century saw pillars become clustered and decorated and rise to fine pointed arches and it is here that we see the first church spire – the type described as broach. Much Early English work is hidden away inside our churches and is not always easy to distinguish. However, the nave, chancel, porch and centre stage of the tower at Cuckney are good examples as are the tower and arcades at Headon. Much of the interior of the churches at Laxton and North Collingham are also of this period and further examples are to be found at Rampton, South Collingham, South Leverton, South Scarle, at Stokeham and Tuxford.

During the 14th century, we have a period called **Decorated**. Here everything is rich and elaborate. Window decorations become ornate, pillars become more slender and parapets and pinnacles appear. Spires become more ornate and are often of the 'recessed' variety. There are beautiful examples of the Decorated style at Edwinstowe, Laxton, South Anston and South Collingham

The final stage of the Medieval building process was in the 15th century when we have the **Perpendicular** period. Here, everything reaches for the sky and everything is light and bright. The clerestory is introduced to give the church interior more light and windows became lofty and wide. The Perpendicular church might be classed as the 'typical' North Nottinghamshire style, noted for its fine towers, often decorated with battlements and pinnacles and the added clerestory. Practically every church on our itineraries will have examples of Perpendicular work with perhaps the finest example being that at East Markham.

The next architectural stage of interest in north Nottinghamshire is that of the 18th century, where brick is often used for the structure which has now become austere with simple round-headed windows piercing a simple box. The best example of such work in our area is at West Stockwith, but the church at Ollerton is also of this time.

The Victorians, apart from carrying out major restorations or even rebuilds of many of the original Medieval structures, introduced a **Gothic**

revival of there own, erecting new buildings in the Medieval style, some of them very good imitations. Amongst these are Thorney (built in the early Norman style), Harby (Early English), Grove and Shireoaks (Decorated), Bothamsall (Perpendicular) and the estate churches at Clumber and Scofton. Finally, we have the modern churches at Besthorpe (1844), Creswell (actually in Derbyshire and dating from 1899-1927), St Anne's at Worksop (built 1911/1912 in the Perpendicular style) and Holbeck (built in the Norman style in 1915).

As already mentioned, few churches could be described as of a single period and throughout their lives have been constantly 'improved'. For instance, Church Warsop has a Norman lower tower, Early English south door, porch and south arcade, Decorated north arcade, Perpendicular clerestory, chantry and tower topping. Cuckney is a mixture of Norman, Early English and Perpendicular styles. South Collingham has a Norman north arcade, Early English lower tower stages, Decorated chancel and Perpendicular clerestory and tower top, while South Scarle has Norman, Early English and Perpendicular work.

Thus, visiting the churches along the walks, our journeys will become ones of exploration as we try to solve the story of the magnificent living history that forms the nucleus of many of the villages we visit. We hope that you will enjoy the walks as much as we have and find the churches as fascinating as we have done.

1. Worksop – Chesterfield Canal – Scofton

Distance: 9½ miles (15km)

Maps: OS Landranger 120: Mansfield & Worksop, Sherwood Forest. OS Explorer 28: Sherwood Forest (to be renumbered 270); 279: Doncaster, Conisbrough, Maltby & Thorne

Start: Memorial Avenue Car Park (adjacent to the Public Library/Museum (GR 587790). This is a 'Pay and Display' facility and it is suggested that the long stay section is used!

Churches: Priory Church of St Mary and St Cuthbert, Worksop; Estate church, Scofton

The Walk

We begin our wanderings in the capital of Bassetlaw District and continue onwards to sample much of what our later strolls will include. A visit to the museum housed with the public library adjacent to the car park will give an insight into the Mayflower Story – a subject we shall be touching on in later walks. The magnificent Priory church is a one-off , but is a fitting start to our journey around the churches of the area. We walk a section of the Chester-field Canal, a feature that will accompany us on many of our later excur-sions. Then there is a fine church – perhaps not quite representative of the North Nottinghamshire style but very much a place of peace and tranquil-lity, like many more we shall visit later. We continue along green lanes which provide many of the links between the villages in this book and finally, a bit of town walking – thankfully, not so common in later walks.

Worksop is described as The Gateway to the Dukeries; it is also the District centre for Bassetlaw. It is a bustling place, heavily influenced by the arrival of the Chesterfield Canal in 1772, the railway in 1849 and the opening of nearby Manton coalpit in 1898. In Domesday Book, the name is spelt 'Werchesope', which comes from the Old English meaning 'the enclosure or valley of a man named Weorc'. (An alternative derivation tracing the name back to Old Scandinavian meaning 'fortified hill' is doubtful). Unfortu-nately, most of its older and more interesting buildings have disappeared, though the façade of the Town Hall, built in 1851 as the Corn Exchange and, close by, the Old Ship inn which, although heavily restored, comes from the 15th/16th centuries, are of note. There are several fine Georgian and Victorian structures, a couple of relatively modern churches (one of which we shall visit in Walk 30) and the mound of an old castle (also a Walk 30 visit). Today though, we shall be taking in what are perhaps Worksop's three most famous sites – the Priory, the Priory Gatehouse and Pickford's Depository.

The Priory Church of St Mary and St Cuthbert, Worksop

The Route

1. Walk to the south-east corner of the car park but instead of passing onto Memorial Avenue, go left through the gated gap and into the grounds of the library/museum. Follow the paved way with Memorial Avenue running parallel over to your right and the museum/library to the left.

Through the hedges to the right can be seen the magnificent War Memorial, which sits in the middle of Memorial Avenue and ahead, the twin towers of the Priory, can be glimpsed behind the trees. On the grass to the right is a memorial commemorating those from the town who gave their lives in The Great War. In 1919, it was decided that the town's war memorial should take the form of an extension to Victoria Hospital and the provision of a memorial in a public place. The monument in Memorial Avenue was unveiled and the hospital extension opened in May 1925. The hospital itself was demolished in 1996, but the original foundation stones and a gable stone were retained and were reset here in continuing remembrance.

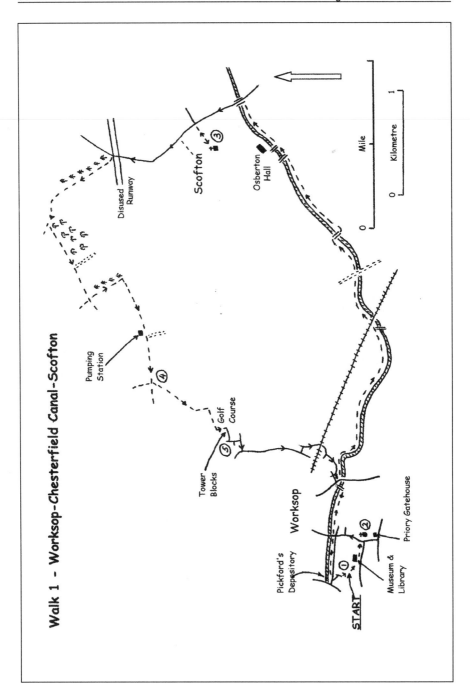

Walk 1 - Worksop-Chesterfield Canal-Scofton

Continue through the park and its extension to emerge via a gateway onto (Priorswell) road with the Priory church opposite and, up to the right, its gatehouse.

The Priory Church of St Mary and St Cuthbert was originally known as Radford Priory since it stood in a separate township of that name which, in later years, became incorporated into the borough of Worksop. It is a fine sleek building with slim dual Norman towers topped with Perpendicular battlements and corner-crocketed pinnacles. Unfortunately, the overall effect is ruined by a modern eastern extension incorporating a spire. The church that we see today is all that remains of the Augustinian Priory established in 1103 by Sir William de Lovetot, Lord of the Manor. The nave was completed by 1170 and originally stretched for 360ft (the current length is a mere 135ft). The western front and towers also date from this period (although the battlements and pinnacles are later). In 1240, Maud Furnival, heiress to Worksop Manor financed the building of the Early English Lady Chapel. John de Tickhill was Prior here from 1303 to 1313 and it was during his time that the illuminated Worksop Psalter, now in the New York Library, was executed. Worksop Priory suffered the fate of all such institutions during the Dissolution, but Worksop was luckier than most for, although all the monastic buildings were destroyed, the main priory church (today's nave) was allowed to remain, though much reduced in size. Restoration was carried out in the 1920s and 1930s and additions were made to the east end in the 1970s. Inside, this is a beautiful light and airy building with magnificent late Norman pillars running the length of the nave and supporting the triforium and clerestory. For such an important building, there are few monuments to be found. The most notable are the battered effigies of Sir Thomas Neville, who was High Treasurer of England and who died in 1404, his wife Joan (died in 1395) and her brother Lord Thomas Furnival ('The Hasty') who was Lord Treasurer of England and who died in 1366. The Priory Gatehouse is a magnificent 14th-century structure, comprising of a central archway with rooms to either side and a main hall above. The façade is striking, especially the large Perpendicular central window flanked by niches containing much worn statues. More lavish however, is the slightly larger porch to the shrine and Lady Chapel. The south-east corner has a decorated projection which was a shrine probably containing a holy relic. It is claimed that the main hall of the gatehouse was used as an elementary school as early as 1628, which would make it the first such school to be established in England. It continued as a school until the 1960s. Before the gatehouse stands the remains of the old market cross which was moved here from its original place opposite the church gates.

2. Return to Priorswell Road and go right, crossing the River Ryton and passing Shelley Street to your right. At Garside Street, cross the road with care and keeping the wall of the canal bridge to your right, descend to the towpath. Go right, walking beneath the bridge (No 43), with the canal to your left. Passing beside Bracebridge Lock, walk onto a narrow road immediately before Bridge No 44, to go left, over the bridge then right to rejoin the towpath but with the canal now to your right. A few metres on we pass beneath the concrete road bridge (No 44A) and stay with the canal as it wends its way to cross the River Ryton.

We pass Kilton Lock and stay with the towpath as it meanders its way over the Ryton again, dips beneath Bridge No 45, the (unnumbered) railway bridge and a Bailey-type bridge (also unnumbered). We cross the canal at the next bridge (No 46) then drop down onto the towpath and continue with the canal now to our left passing beneath bridges 47 and 48.

Over the canal to the left, we get a view of Osberton Hall and the stable block with its cupola clock tower. This was the home of the Foljambe family who acquired the estate in the 18ᵗʰ century but of their lovely house, nothing remains. A replacement was erected here in 1806 but this was virtually rebuilt in 1877. Today, the estate is probably best known for its annual horse trials and we shall soon be walking part of the course as well as visiting the estate church which sits at the edge of the tiny settlement of Scofton.

Passing beside Osberton Lock, we emerge onto a lane at Bridge No 49 and go left, over the bridge and canal. Stay with the lane as its crosses the River Ryton and, at the 'centre' of the settlement of Scofton where a surfaced lane goes off to the right, go left onto a path between cottages and so to the beautifully isolated church.

Scofton is one of those little places which are rarely found by the normal traveller. In fact, it is difficult to reach unless you walk this walk! It revolved around nearby Osberton Hall, and the church is beautifully sited in a field at the edge of the village and over the lake and river from the Hall. It is a relatively modern estate church built for George Savile Foljambe in 1833, the date clearly carved in the wall at the east end. There is a sturdy tower capped with battlements and massive corner pinnacles, a combined nave and chancel, aisles and clerestory. All here is ashlar and mock Norman with some fine carvings including an owl and a pussycat at the west door. Despite its close relationship to the Hall, the early tombs of the Foljambe family are to be found at Chesterfield.

3. Return to Scofton 'centre' and go left, up the lane. Pass through a wide gateway and at the three-way finger-post, go forward through a bridlegate beside fieldgates and gently mount the wide lane with its massive verges (used for the horse trials). Stay with the main surfaced way as it curves to the right and arrive at the edge of the old airfield (now used for vehicle testing). Go directly over (watch out for traffic!) and at

the far side, *do not continue along the metalled lane* but go left onto a track with a thin screen of conifer woodland to your right and hedge to the left. Our track, a wide green swathe, bends to the left and drops into a shallow valley.

At the bottom, leave the lovely grassy gallop and go left onto a waymarked track, which keeps to the edge of woodland to our left. Continue forward at the end of the woodland and pick up a thick hedge to the left. At a T-junction (in fact, a minor path continues through a kissing gate here) with fenceline/gate ahead, go left, up-slope, with the main track. Soon, we pick up a strip of conifers to the left and, where the way ahead is barred by a gateway, go right, still with the main track, which rises gently between fences. We pass a water pumping station to our right and, ignoring the track going off to the left, continue with the main rising track with a hedge to the left. 600m beyond the pumping station and just before arriving at the top of the slope, look out for a hedgeline coming in from the right with a track going off with it. Here we leave the main way.

4. Go diagonally left over the field, aiming to the left of three stunted tower-blocks which can be seen in the distance, soon dropping down to the bottom field corner with golf course beyond. Pass through the gap here and go sharply to the left along the edge of the golf course and keeping close to the hedge on your left. A couple of hundred metres on, look out for painted bollards of pink and blue where we go right and, using those ahead as our markers, cross the greens (look out for flying golf balls!). At the far side of the golf course, go left, with garden fences to your right and, immediately beyond the first of the tower blocks, go right onto a surfaced path between low railings and emerge onto the end of a cul-de-sac (Osberton View).

5. Continue to a T-junction (Browning Close) and go left. Pass Kipling Close to your right and, at the next T-junction (Coleridge Road), go right to a major junction (Plantation Hill). Go left, down the slope, passing a host of writers and, eventually, The Lord Byron inn to the left. Pass Sitwell Road to the left then take the next left (Rayton Spur), which bends to the right and drops to curve right again and pass beneath a railway bridge. Following the road round beyond the bridge, go left along Bracebridge Avenue and stay with it as it eventually bends to the right to arrive at a crossroads (with Bracebridge). Go left here and immediately before the busy High Hoe Road, go left down a surfaced pathway, which drops to the canal towpath. Go right, beneath the road bridge (No 44A)

and retrace the route described in Section 1 as far as Bridge No 43 where we originally joined the canal at the start of our walk.

The church spire which can been seen in the distance ahead is that of St John, a Victorian building not visited on our walks.

Stay forward with the towpath here (you may be forced onto the adjacent road by fishing rods, but, where the iron railings begin, try and keep them to your left with the canal immediately to the right). Soon, ahead, is the old Pickford's Depository, now a popular bar.

During the early 19th century, the Chesterfield Canal was an extremely busy waterway and the depository, spanning the canal in the centre of the town was typical of the time. It is a three-storey building with small upper windows but large loading doors on the ground and first floors. These were used to admit cargoes, which would then be lowered through trap doors in the archway and into the narrow-boats in the canal below.

At the end of the railings, go left onto the road (The Canal Tavern is over the road to the left) and then right. Take the first left (Church Walk) and at the T-junction with the Fisherman's Arms on the corner, go right. At the end of the cul-de-sac, continue along a surfaced pathway which swings left and right over two small river footbridges and so back to the car park and the start of our walk.

2. Shireoaks – Chesterfield Canal – South Anston – Lindrick Dale

Distance: 7¾ miles (12.5km)

Maps: OS Landranger Sheet: 120 Mansfield & Worksop, Sherwood Forest. OS Explorer 279: Doncaster; Conisbrough, Maltby & Thorne

Start: St Luke's church, Shireoaks (GR 554809). Ample parking at the Village Hall, Shireoaks Road, behind the church. Please check with the key holder if more than a couple of cars are to use this facility.

Churches: St Luke, Shireoaks; St James, South Anston

The Walk

Our second walk begins in Nottinghamshire but swiftly moves into South Yorkshire to follow a lovely stretch of the Chesterfield Canal (where, at the time of writing, the bridges are unfortunately unnumbered). A short uphill field section takes us to South Anston and its fine church. We return via some beautiful heath and woodland before passing through the delightful Lindrick Dale, skirting the golf course, then rejoining the canal towpath back to Shireoaks.

Shireoaks does not appear in Domesday Book but, in the 12th century, we have 'Shirakes', a name coming from the Old English meaning 'the oak trees on the (county) border'. The trees themselves stood to the south of the village, close to the Nottinghamshire-Derbyshire-Yorkshire border and are marked on maps at GR 534789. The village was once a busy mining centre, the colliery, the first deep pit in the County, being opened in 1845 by the 4th Duke of Newcastle and it was his son who financed the building of the church. Little remains of the original structure of Shireoaks Hall, built by Henry Hewett in about 1600, but there still exist the magnificent water gardens for which Henry's grandson, Sir Thomas Hewett, Surveyor General to George I, was responsible. St Luke's is a fine example of a 19th-century church built in the Decorated style. It comprises of a centrally placed tower with large external staircase, nave, apsidal chancel and aisles, protrusions from the base of the tower giving the impression of transepts. The building was financed by the 5th Duke of Newcastle and the foundation stone was laid by the Prince of Wales (later Edward VII) in 1861, William Gladstone, then Chancellor of the Exchequer, dedicating the East window. The church was finally consecrated on St Luke's Day in 1863. Originally, the tower supported a spire but this was removed in 1975 when it became unsafe due to mining subsidence.

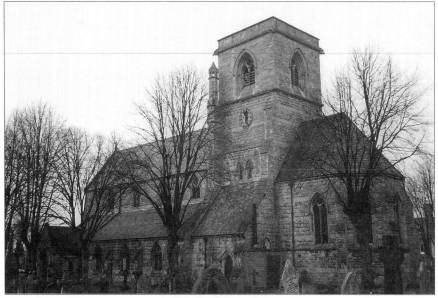

St Luke, Shireoaks

The Route

1. Leave the church by the gates which lead onto Shireoaks Row and go left with the church building to your left. A few metres on, where the road swings left as Shireoaks Road, cross, to go right onto a lane signed as 'leading to Bethel Terrace'. Pass the Terrace to your right (the old Primitive Methodist chapel dated 1891 is to the left) and continue forward through a metal barrier. We pass beside the sports ground entrance and our lane, now a gravel and stone track, meanders with fishing lake over a fence to the right. Where the main track swings right to a gateway, go forward along a lesser pathway between trees and bushes to arrive on the bank of the Chesterfield Canal with a lock-up to your right. Bear left along the bank (canal to the right) to a recently restored brick bridge which we mount to cross the canal and then drop down left to rejoin the towpath with a lock and the waterway now to our left.

2. Stay on the towpath, soon entering the tiny hamlet of Turnerwood and, passing beneath the road bridge here, continue for a little over half a mile, eventually arriving at another red brick bridge. Pass beneath this

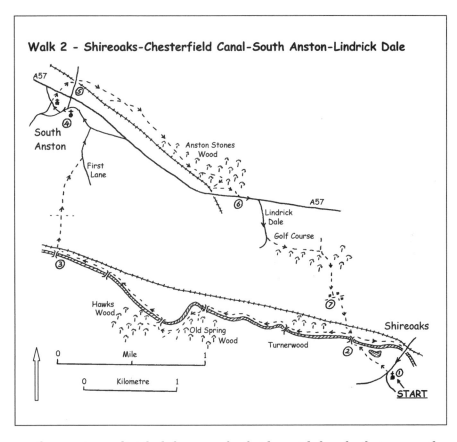

Walk 2 - Shireoaks-Chesterfield Canal-South Anston-Lindrick Dale

then go immediately left over a footbridge with handrails to cross the canal and go forward into Old Spring Wood. With the Wood notice board to your left, go right on a woodland path with the canal visible through the trees to the right. Our path meanders through the trees and about 50m before a field gate ahead and opposite another Old Spring Wood sign, go right over a waymarked stile in a section of fence. Continue through the trees to another stile, which takes us onto a farm track. Go right down the track, passing sewage works to your left and, ignoring the finger-posted path to the left, stay with the main route which drops gently to the gated entrance to Hawks Wood. Do not go through the gate but follow the track round to the right to cross the canal and rejoin the towpath. Continue along the canal bank with the waterway to your left, passing beneath another bridge and, immediately before the next bridge, leave the canal to go right passing through a wicket gate which takes us over the railway line.

3. Continue forward over a small stream then mount through a thick hedge to a field edge. Continue the line gently upwards between fields, crossing a farm track and soon picking up a hedge to your right. Our route bends through a hedge gap and we continue with the hedge now to our left and soon, the houses of Anston ahead. Passing beside garden hedges and fences to our left we arrive at a minor road (First Lane) where we go left to the B6059. Go left along the pavement, gently meandering downwards into the outskirts of South Anston (cross the road to the pavement on the far side where ours comes to an end then cross again) to find the steps into the grounds of St James.

Anston today is cut in half by the A57 trunk road but even in Domesday Book, the existence of two separate settlements is recognised for we have both 'Anestan' and 'Litelanstan'. By 1297, these had become Northanstan and Suthanstan, the root name coming from the Old English meaning 'the solitary stone' (we shall soon pass plenty of stony outcrops). The church of St James is a beautifully proportioned building with 15th-century battlemented tower, complete with corner-crocketed pinnacles and capped by a fine recessed spire. This lovely building is somewhat spoiled by the addition of a modern church hall which has been stuck onto the 15th-century south porch and which looks totally out of place. The oldest part of the church is the nave, which dates to the 12th century. From a hundred years later come the aisles, while the chancel (of which the original roofline can be seen in the wall of the nave) is 14th century. Behind the relatively modern octagonal font is one of the most interesting church monuments in South Yorkshire – a much worn but magnificent stone carving depicting the praying figures of an adult and child, possibly a father and daughter, dating from the 14th century.

4. Leave the church by the path which leads from the base of the tower and through a fine stone archway onto the road. Go left for a few metres then *bear right, (not sharply right)* dropping down into the village, and passing the Loyal Trooper inn to your right then the Leeds Arms to the left. On the right now we have the impressive modern Methodist church with its square tower and Norman-style doorway and windows, with, next to it, the old Wesleyan Methodist Hall with the date 1871. Immediately beyond the Hall, go right down a narrow alleyway (Chapel Walk) and, keeping hedge/garden wall to your right, arrive on the busy A57. Cross the road with care and continue forward down another alley with garages to your right. The path drops between fences/hedges then does a sharp turn to the right to arrive on a road.

5. Go left, passing beneath the railway bridge then almost immediately right down a finger-posted path which dips to a footbridge over a stream.

Cross and follow the path round to the right with the stream to your right. Soon we leave the stream as our path mounts over grassland to a track crossing. Go right here on a stony path with the valley down to the right and hedgeline to the left, soon passing between hedges and trees and continuing through scrubland. Stay with the main path (another path comes in obliquely from the right) and at a Y-junction, just beyond a large pitted boulder to your right, take the left branch, going gently up-slope, climbing stone steps onto heathland. We pass rock outcrops and, still with the main path, walk parallel to an old stone wall over to our right before passing through a gap in the wall and going left into the trees.

We are now in the beautiful Anston Stones Wood which covers an area of some 83 acres and is described as the finest limestone native woodland in the north of England. The landscape here has been formed by the Anston Brook, which has carved out a magnificent gorge and created a perfect habitat for plants and animals, including man, evidence of whose habitation can be traced back some 10,000 years.

Stay with the main path, which initially keeps close to the wood edge then drops down steps to green railings. *Ignore the continuing steps and go left*, still just within the edge of the woodland now studded with rocky outcrops. Emerging from the trees, continue forward with bushes/hedges to your right then on over a clearing (do not drop down to the right) to re-enter the woods. Follow the main path as it bends right and drops gently to steps with railings. Descend the steps and, at the bottom of the slope, go left over a footbridge to a cross-track with a railway arch to the right. Go left here with the brook down to your left and follow the track as it mounts to emerge through a huge kissing gate and onto the busy A57.

6. Cross the road with care and go left, down slope, keeping within the long lay-by area. A couple of hundred metres on, at the bottom of the slope, go right onto Lindrick Dale (a surfaced lane) where we enter the most delightfully placed little hamlet tucked into a steep sided valley. At the far end of the hamlet, where a track goes off to the right at a three-way finger-post, go forward then, immediately before The Cottage, go left up a stony track with a cliff to your left and The Cottage to the right. At the top of the slope, go forward through metal posts and bear to the right with thick hedges/trees to your right and, screened behind dense vegetation to the left, the golf course. Following the path between trees and bushes we soon arrive at the edge of the greens where we go forward with care, taking the yellow posts as markers, to arrive at a cross track. Go

right here down the finger-posted bridleway to another cross-track. Go left, gently up-slope with a beck down to your left and, following the track as it bears to the right, ignore the stile, gate and path off right. Continue upwards on the main path to emerge from the trees. Continue forward between fields, gently dropping towards farm buildings and eventually passing through a metal field gate with stone stile beside it and so onto a farm lane.

7. Go left along the lane for about 60m then, at the end of a stone wall to your right, go right onto a finger-posted path with the wall initially to your right. Our path bears slightly to the left, leaving the wall and aiming for a gap in the tree line ahead with railway embankment behind. At the far side of the field, cross a stile, mount the steps of the embankment and cross the railway line with care. Descend the far side and cross the stile into a field edge, where we bear diagonally left over the field corner to cross another stile. Then, continue the line to bear right and join the Chesterfield canal at the bridge where we joined it at the start of our walk. Go left along the towpath with the canal to your right, eventually arriving on Shireoaks Row with The Station inn to your left. Leave the canal here to go right along the road, and so back to the church and our start point.

3. Blyth – Hodsock Priory – South Carlton

Distance: 8¾ miles (14km)

Maps: OS Landranger 120: Mansfield & Worksop, Sherwood Forest. OS Explorer 279: Doncaster; Conisbrough, Maltby & Thorne

Start: High Street, Blyth (GR 626869). Limited parking on the 'old' High Street, east of the green. Note that High Street shoppers, local residents and patrons of the White Swan inn use this area, so please park 'prettily'

Churches: St Mary and St Martin, Blyth; St John the evangelist, Carlton in Lindrick

The Walk

Our third walk is anchored firmly in Nottinghamshire, starting at one of its most magnificent churches. We continue over fields to the edge of the Hodsock estate then along green lanes to Carlton in Lindrick. A short section of woodland brings us to the church at South Carlton before our return along field headlands and tracks, which take us through the grounds of Hodsock and so, by surfaced lanes, back to Blyth.

Blyth is spelt 'Blide' in The Domesday Book, taking its name from the river that is nowadays called the Ryton and which we shall be meeting soon. Blyth sprang to importance two years after the compilation of The Domesday Book when, in 1088, its Benedictine Priory was founded by Roger de Busli (or Builli), the Norman overlord of Tickhill. A hundred years later, in 1194, Richard I granted a license for a tournament ground just north of the town and in 1226, William Cressy of Hodsock founded a leper colony here. This was rebuilt in 1446 and the building still survives (as private cottages) at the southern end of the green. Following the Dissolution of the Monasteries by Henry VIII, the Priory's lodging was converted into a residence known as Blyth Abbey and in 1689, the first Blyth Hall was built on the site by Edward Mellish. The Hall was demolished in 1972 but the stable block, built in 1770, remains. In 1806, Colonel Henry Francis Mellish sold the Blyth estate (some say he gambled it away) to Joshua Walker of Rotherham but the family eventually sold the Hall to Francis Willey of Bradford, who became Lord Barnby after the First World War. There are many fine buildings to be seen in the village, the inns being a reminder of its importance as a staging post on The Great North Road. Today, thankfully, there is a bypass and Blyth now nestles away from the heavy traffic.

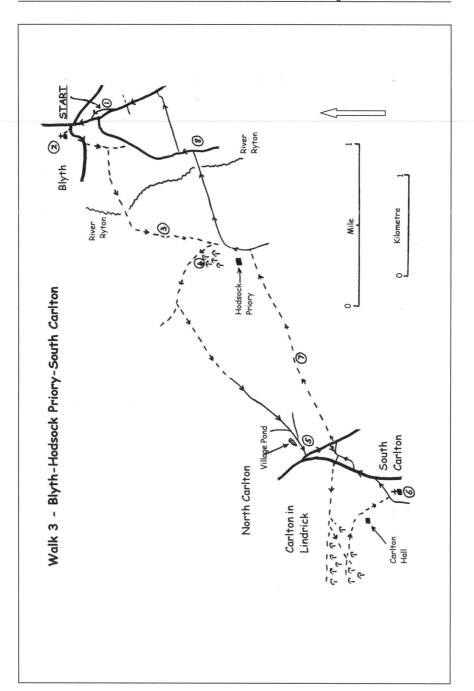

Walk 3 – Blyth–Hodsock Priory–South Carlton

The Route

1. Go northwards along the 'old' High Street towards the great church tower with the village green to your left and the White Swan inn to the right. Continuing along High Street, we have the Wesleyan chapel (1902) over the road to the left with, next to it, the Barnby Memorial Hall, built by Lord Barnby in thanks for his son's safe return from the First World War and in memory of those who did not do so. Cross Retford Road which goes off to your right then go left, over the busy road and to the patch of greenery at the Sheffield Road junction where a post supports the village arms.

The Blyth Village Sign bears the dates 1088-1988, and celebrates the 900ᵗʰ anniversary of the founding of the church. It is framed in a Norman arch which remembers the founders of the building and in front of a representation of the church tower can be seen nine priors and vicars who represent the nine centuries of the church's history. The jousters (Cliftons and Cressys) are reminders of the tournament field to the north of the village and the swans were the motif found on the Mellish family arms. In the centre, at the bottom, the playing cards refer to the rumour that the Blyth estate was gambled away by Henry Francis Mellish in 1806. Finally, stretched along the base, are the hands of hospitality and friendship which were offered by the original Benedictine monks.

Bear right, up the driveway and into the grounds of the Church of St Mary and St Martin.

Always welcoming and with so much to see and admire, the structure we see now differs markedly from that which existed prior to the Reformation – it lacks its Priory. Today, we have a massive pinnacled tower but instead of battlements, beautiful tracery. There is a huge south porch but the nave looks very strange – truncated – almost unfinished. In fact, the east end was formerly the Priory section and it has been chopped off. The Benedictine Priory was founded in 1088 as a cell of the Abbey of St Cuthbert in Rouen. Dating from this early period, we still have the nave and north aisle with its magnificent Norman pillars. The south aisle was pulled down around 1290 and rebuilt to its current size as the parish church. At the start of the 13ᵗʰ century, the present roof was added to the nave, the line of stones above the clerestory windows showing its original height. Around 1400, Sir Gervaise Clifton had the church rebuilt. At about this time, quarrels between the monks and the parishioners led to the erection of the great wall at the east end of the nave to separate the two, the only access to the Priory being through a small door. To decorate this wall and provide a teaching-aid for parishioners who could not read, the church commissioned a painting of the Last Judgement or Doom, now thought to be one of the largest and most significant in the country.

In 1538, the Priory was finally dissolved, the central tower, the transepts and choir were all pulled down and what was left was claimed by the local villagers as their church. The painting, which was considered out of fashion, was limewashed over; but the lime served as a preservative. In 1703, the successors of Edward Mellish of Blyth Hall had his marble monument erected against the east wall thus hiding the painting completely. However, in the 1885 church refurbishment, the monument was removed to its present position in the north aisle. The East wall was then thought to show some remnants of a painting, but it was left undisturbed, to be finally rediscovered in 1985. There is so much to see in the church and we can only recommend the booklets available for sale and plenty of time. Note especially though, the Mellish memorials and hatchments, the seventeenth-century font, the list of Priors going back to Ascelinus (1133) but which stops abruptly in 1534 and the list of vicars which begins in 1240.

2. Return to Sheffield Road and go right. The road bends to the left, passing the former Rectory topped with its pretty cupola then the old stables which are now converted to modern dwellings and which have an old milestone set into the wall. The road makes a slight bend to the right and with Park Drive to your right and a grey-stone cottage (Park Lodge, with the date 1840) over, cross the road to walk up a finger-posted track between trees. 300m on, go right onto a headland track with a huge power pylon in the field to your left, soon picking up a broken hedge/treeline to your right. Our path soon drops gently with magnificent views to the front. At the bottom of the slope, go through a gateway (or over adjacent stile) and bear left over a narrow neck of land. Go through the bridlegate or over the adjacent stile and continue along the headland with hedgeline to your left. Cross the footbridge over the River Ryton and go forward through scrub and the remains of willow woodland to emerge onto a field corner. Continue with a ditch to your left and, 20m before the corner of the field, go left through the finger-posted hedge gap (beside an old stone bollard). Bear diagonally right up the field, aiming for a hedge gap ahead to pass through the gap and continue the line and arrive on a farm track with a hedge beyond.

3. Go forward through a hedge gap and bear left over the field aiming for a stile in the far hedge. [Note that diversions are sometimes placed here which necessitate going left along the track with the hedge to your right for a short distance then bearing right to the stile. If these are in use, they will be marked]. Cross the stile and continue forward with fence to your right. [Note: at the end of the fence, our route onwards is down to the right, to the point where Horse Pasture Wood joins the field corner. Unfortunately, there is no legal direct link between these two points, and thus a dogleg must be followed]. At the end of the fence, bear slightly to

the right, walking down the field and aiming for a set of double fieldgates. (There is another set of gates further to the left – we do not want these). *Do not pass through the gates but turn your back on them* and walk diagonally left back over the field, with woodland to your left, and aiming for the point where the wood meets the top field corner.

4. Here, go left through a gateway and onto a green lane with woodland to the left. Soon we are walking between hedges then pass through a gap onto a headland track with a hedge to our right. After 80m, at a junction, bear left, with a hedge to the right and continue with occasional distant glimpses to the front left of South Carlton church tower. Our track eventually becomes a wide hedged green lane then, a narrow surfaced road. To the right we pass the attractive village duckpond and picnic area (a good place for a rest) then, on the left, the old pinfold (now a vegetable plot), finally to emerge onto the road in Carlton in Lindrick.

5. Go left, dropping gently, then take the first right (The Cross) into the centre of the old village. Continue forward with The Grey Horses Inn to your right then follow the main road round to the right and so onto High Road with the Wesleyan chapel (1861) on the corner to your left. Cross with care, to follow a footpath signed 'to Wallingwells 1¼' which passes initially between garden fences/hedges to enter Carlton Wood. Go forward into the trees, ignoring the first track off to the left and after about 100m, bear left at a junction onto a well-trodden path which takes us deeper into the woodland. 250m on, at a cross track amongst yews and rhododendrons, go left again beneath yew trees, and follow the path out of the wood and onto a headland path with a hedge to your right. Soon we pick up the wall of a lovely converted farmhouse (Carlton Hall Farm) to our right and follow this perimeter closely to a bridlegate into field. Cross the field, aiming directly for the church tower ahead, passing through another bridlegate, over another stretch of grassland and through a wall gap and onto a lane with the church opposite.

In Domesday Book, Carlton in Lindrick is simply 'Carletone', a common place name in areas subjected to the Danelaw and meaning 'the farmstead/estate of freemen'. The suffix first appears in 1212 and comes from the old district name which itself is Old English and means 'the strip of land where lime trees grow'. Today, in addition to Carlton in Lindrick, we have North Carlton (previously known as Kingston-in-Carlton) and South Carlton (previously Carlton Baron). At first sight, the church of St John the Evangelist looks very much like a normal North Nottinghamshire 15th-century Perpendicular building. But this is not the case. It is the tower that makes the difference for, once below the Perpendicular upper stage, we are into what is probably the best Saxon/Norman tower in

St John the Evangelist, Carlton in Lindrick

Nottinghamshire. This tower is magnificent! There is an abundance of herringbone work and the west door is a Norman beauty. Inside the church are a fine 11th-century tower arch, a Norman north arcade and a lovely Norman font. Although appearing ancient, the south arcade dates from 1831 when there was a major restoration and the south aisle was added (the Norman west doorway was moved to its present position from a south porch at the time of this restoration).

6. Return to the lane and go right, to arrive on the A60 with the war memorial cross to your right. Go left, crossing this busy road as quickly as possible. Pass the primary school over to the left and, 100m on, go right into Low Street. Continue into the old village, passing the Grey Horses Inn to your left, then, at the little triangle where we came in from the front earlier, bear right to Greenway (road). Cross with care – this is a blind bend – to go left, up the slope, for about 20m then right, onto a finger-posted path between walls. Cross a stile and go forward with garden fences right and ignoring the waymarked path to the left, continue to another stile. Cross the field and yet another stile to pick up a headland path with a hedge to your left. At the next field corner, cross the stile and continue the line, still with the hedge to the left. Where the hedge bends sharply to the left, go forward over a narrow neck of land to cross a final stile onto a major track.

7. Bear right and ignoring all side routes, continue along the main track, Hodsock Priory eventually coming into view to the front left.

    The 'Priory' was never a monastic building but there was once a large 13ᵗʰ-century moated manor house here. The property passed from the Cressy family to the Cliftons who used it as an alternative to Clifton Hall. Later it was the home of the Mellish family when their estate at Blyth was lost. What we see today is a 16ᵗʰ-century gatehouse leading to an early 19ᵗʰ-century mock-Tudor residence. There were additions to the building in the 1870s and fine gardens have been formed which are opened to the public in the spring, when there is a wonderful display of snowdrops to be seen.

    Continue to a T-junction and go left along the surfaced lane, passing the guesthouse complex to your left, then with fine views of the Priory and gatehouse. Follow the lane as it bends to the right and continue forward until you recross the River Ryton and mount to the busy B6045.

8. Go left along the road (cross as quickly as possible to the footway in the grass verge), then, 200m on, go right onto a finger-posted surfaced lane signed as a Private Road to Spital Farm. Stay with the lane as it climbs gently with, soon, views of Blyth church far to the left. Follow the lane as it passes between farm buildings and bears left to drop onto Spital Road and the outskirts of Blyth. Go left down into the village and at the bottom of the slope bear right onto the 'old' High Street (named Spital Road at its start) and thus back to our start point beside the green.

    Don't pass the Green with too much haste, there is plenty of history to be found here. At the southern end, note especially all that remains of the Medieval leper colony buildings, now private cottages. The building is responsible for the name 'spital' (hospital) which we have met recently. Beyond is a cairn in memory of the crew of a Wellington bomber of RAF Worksop, which crashed near here on 7ᵗʰ March 1944. One of the crew members survived but, sadly, was killed in action in August of the same year. The cairn also carries the names of seven members of the Canadian Airforce killed when their Halifax bomber crashed at Hodsock on 2ⁿᵈ August, 1944.

4. Serlby – Scrooby – Ranskill – Roman Bank

Distance: 8 miles (13km)

Maps: OS Landranger 111: Sheffield & Doncaster, Barnsley & Thorne. OS Explorer 279: Doncaster; Conisbrough, Maltby & Thorne

Start: Serlby (GR 643892). Ample parking on verges at the southern end of Green Lane opposite the northern end of the Roman Bank bridleway.

Churches: St Wilfred, Scrooby; St Barnabas, Ranskill

The Walk

A stroll along green lanes, between lakes and among the trees of Roman Bank. There are a couple of sections of road-walking but these are relatively short. We take in the church at Scrooby, closely linked to that at Babworth (Walk 11) and the Mayflower story and visit the little modern building of St Barnabas, Ranskill.

Serlby is best known today for its golf course but, in the past, was better known for the wonderful structure of Serlby Hall. The estate was purchased by the first Viscount Galway in 1727 and it was his successor who began construction of a fine country mansion here in the 1750s. The present house, which can just be glimpsed through the trees, is a rebuild of 1812. The whole is surrounded by beautiful grounds that include a mound where it is believed the church of a now lost village once stood.

The Route

1. Walk northwards on the green lane (at the time of writing, a Permissive Path, which it is hoped will become a permanent Public Right of Way in the near future) with the golf practice area through the bushes and trees to your left. Stay with the main track with glimpses of the tower of Harworth Colliery in the distance to the left. Our path soon bends to the right and rises gently to a crest where we get our first glimpse of the spire of Scrooby church in the distance to our left. Stay with the main track, which drops gently to pass through a metal half-gate onto the busy A638.

2. Cross with care to the pavement on the far side and go left along the road and entering the outskirts of Scrooby. Ignore a finger-posted bridleway to the right and continue with the main road as it curves to the left where we go forward onto Low Road and so to the church of St Wilfrid.

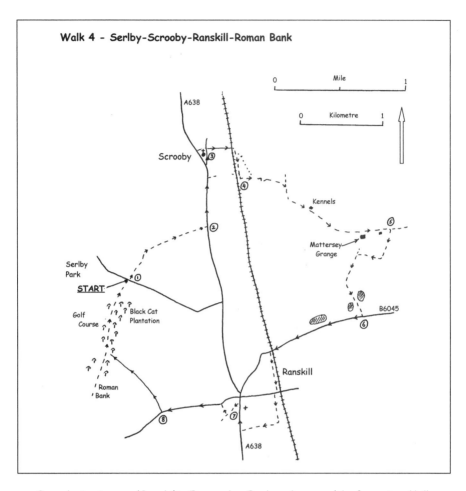

Walk 4 - Serlby-Scrooby-Ranskill-Roman Bank

Scrooby is given as 'Scrobi' in Domesday Book and means 'the farmstead/village of Skropi', presumably a local Viking. However, the earliest mention is as Scroppenthorp in 958 when King Edgar granted land here to the Archbishop of York. From this began a long association with the archbishops who established a 'palace' (or manor house) here. King John stayed briefly in 1212, in 1530 Cardinal Wolsey was a visitor, and eleven years later, Henry VIII held a Privy Council at the manor. Soon though, the manor building fell into ruin and was virtually demolished in the 1630s. In 1750, a major renovation was carried out and this is the building that can be found today. Scrooby is best known though as the birthplace of William Brewster (in around 1566) who, with the Reverend Richard Clyfton of nearby Babworth (see Walk 11) and William Bradford, from Austerfield (Yorkshire), formed a Separatist church here in 1606. The following year, Brewster and a number of his friends left England to escape religious persecution and went first to Holland, then in 1620, crossed the Atlantic in the Mayflower to found the Colony of New England. He died there in 1644. A church is mentioned here as early as 1177 but of this old building nothing remains. St Wilfrid's is a Perpendicular building with a north Nottinghamshire rarity – a 15th-century spire, recessed and mounted on a battlemented and pinnacled tower with strange rounded corners. There is a combined nave and chancel, a south aisle, added in the 16th century, and a 14th-century (restored) south porch. There was a major restoration in 1864 and most of the internal fittings date from this time.

3. Leave the church by the north-west gate, noting the pinfold to the left, and go right along Church Lane with the church to your right. At the cross-roads, go forward and continue down Station Road. Cross the railway line with care, making use of the stiles to either side of the track and, at the far side, go right along a grassy path with a beck and the railway to your right and a field fence to the left. [Note: A path, denoted by a stile, leads diagonally over the field to your left. This provides a slightly shorter route but the field is frequently used to graze cattle and rather than disturb them, the described path is the preferred one]. Cross a culvert and continue with the ditch now down to your left. A bridleway comes in from the right but we continue forward to go left over a bridleway bridge a few metres before metal field gates.

4. Our path follows the field edge with a fence to the left, passing a stile which marks the other end of the 'short-cut'. At the field corner, with a deep ditch ahead, go right for a few metres then left over another bridleway bridge. On the far side of the bridge, bear left with a large marshy pond surrounded by trees and bushes to the right then bear right along the headland with scattered bushes and trees to your left. Arriving on a farm track, go right and follow it as it bends to the left to pass a cattery and kennels then, after about another half mile, pass between the buildings of Mattersey Grange (farm).

5. Continue along the track, passing a cottage with the date 1873 to your right then, about 120m on, go right through a wide hedge gap onto a finger-posted headland path with a hedge to your right. Follow the hedge as it bends to the right to arrive on a farm access track with Mattersey Grange up to the right. Go left here, along the stony track, which passes beside (private) woodland then meanders between lakes to emerge onto Ranskill Road (the B6045).

6. Go right along the road (taking great care since there is no pavement and the verges are minimal), arriving after about fifteen minutes at the outskirts of Ranskill. Cross the railway bridge then, a few metres on,

St Barnabas, Ranskill

leave the road to go left onto a surfaced pathway paralleling the railway which is in a cutting to your left and with house gardens right. Arriving on a road with level crossing to the left, go right for 100m, passing a garage, and immediately beyond Harcourt House with the date 1899 to your left, go left onto Headland Lane. The lane deteriorates to a dirt track, soon giving us views over to the right of the little bellcoted church of St Barnabas. Follow the track as it bends sharply to the right and follow it to emerge onto the Great North Road. Go right along the pavement to the church.

Ranskill appears as 'Raveschel' in Domesday Book. The meaning is not entirely clear but it could be either 'the shelf or ridge frequented by ravens' or 'the ridge of a man called Hrafn', the latter being an Old Scandinavian personal name. Today, the village straddles the Great North Road and is usually missed in the rush from Retford to Bawtry and beyond. There are though, some interesting buildings, including the 1891 Reading Room, a fine inn and the modern looking church of St Barnabas which is well worth a short visit. The little stone building with red tiled roof is a Ewan Christian construction dating from 1878. It comprises a simple but lofty nave, lower chancel, south porch and single slim bellcote mounted to the south-west of the building. Inside, all is plain and light. There is a lovely wooden roof and a modern and plain octagonal font set on an older inscribed base.

7. Return to the road and go right for about 100m then go left onto Back Lane. Follow the main track as it swings to the right (not the green lane going left), passing beside a brick wall to your right and emerging through a metal gate onto the Blyth Road. Go left along the road for about half a mile (there is a pavement all the way), leaving the village behind and soon gaining distant views ahead of Blyth church tower. Pass a couple of isolated cottages to your right then, where the road bends to the left (with large black and white warning arrows for vehicles), go right onto a narrow metalled lane.

8. Pass a lone cottage to your right and continue forward with the tower of Harworth Colliery in the distance ahead. A few metres before a metal gateway bars progress, go right at a finger-posted cross-track onto a lovely path. This is a northern extension of the embankment known as Roman Bank, which hugs the edge of woodland with the golf course through the trees to your left. Stay with the main path as it rises gently then levels to pass Black Cat Plantation to the right then drops to arrive on a lane with our start point opposite.

5. Mattersey – Everton – Barrow Hills

Distance: 7 miles (11.3km)

Maps: OS Landranger 111: (Sheffield & Doncaster; Barnsley & Thorne. OS Explorer 279: Doncaster; Conisbrough, Maltby & Thorne

Start: Mattersey church (GR 691894). Limited parking (especially at church service times) in the lay-by on Abbey Road immediately south of church. Additional, but very limited parking can be found at the end of Church Lane south of the River Idle.

Churches: All Saints, Mattersey; Holy Trinity, Everton

The Walk

Crossing the River Idle and following a short section of metalled track we cross Eel Pool Lane to climb gently through lovely woodland then drop by green lane to the outskirts of Everton. Access track and field paths bring us into the village and its magnificent church. Our route continues to the hamlet of Harwell where we climb again to the wonderful ridge path through the trees of Barrow Hills before descending to the busy A631. A short section of road walking leads to a series of green lanes and finally more woodland to bring us back to our start point.

Mattersey is given as 'Madressei' in Domesday Book, coming from the Old English meaning 'the island or the well-watered land of a man called Maethhere'. Mattersey is perhaps best known for its Gilbertine priory, which lies at the very end of Abbey Road, a one-mile walk or bumpy drive east of the village. The priory, founded in 1185, was destroyed by fire in 1279, quickly rebuilt but dissolved in 1538. It was never a rich foundation and had only six canons when it was established and five on dissolution. Today, there is little to be seen apart from sections of dormitory and refectory walls together with the remains of its 15th-century chapel dedicated to St Helen. The two-mile return journey along the same track makes this site difficult to incorporate into a circular walk but a drive there would make a fine conclusion to today's stroll. All Saints was granted to Mattersey priory in 1280 but little of the original building remains. What we see today is a typical North Nottinghamshire Perpendicular church comprising of a battlemented tower with corner-crocketed pinnacles, nave, chancel, north and south aisles, clerestory and south porch. The wall of the north aisle is magnificently decorated with fantastic gargoyles and these are carried on to the tower. Inside, there are examples of variously dated architecture including 14th-century

All Saints, Mattersey

nave arcades and a 13th-century chancel arcade. Most lovely though are two 14th-century carved panels, one showing St Martin, the other, St Helen, and these are thought to have originated in the priory. A 19th-century restoration was, fortunately, completed with taste and left this lovely building largely unspoiled.

The Route

1. Leave the church by the south gateway and go right then immediately right again into Church Lane with the Barley Mow inn to your left and then the church up to the right. Leaving the village houses behind, cross the River Idle by the footbridge (alternative car parking) and continue along the pitted tarmac track that leads to the B6045 (Eel Pool Lane). Go right for about 100m then cross the road to go left onto the finger-posted bridleway into Pusto Hill Wood. Follow the main track forward up a gentle incline into the trees. At a junction, go forward again, bearing gently to the left to climb more steeply, initially between low embankments, then flattening out to emerge onto Pusto Hill Lane with barns to your right. Go forward along the track and, ignoring side routes, descend gently to the A631.

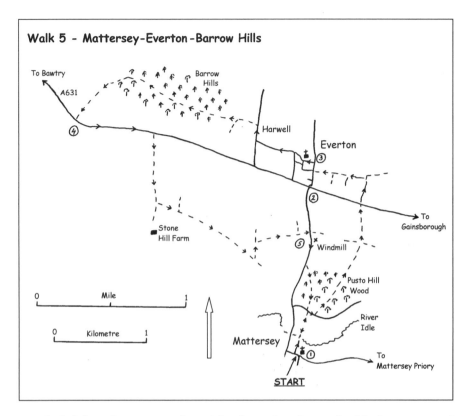

Walk 5 - Mattersey-Everton-Barrow Hills

2. Go left for a few metres then right, (crossing the road with the greatest of care) and taking the finger-posted access track signed 'Nottinghamshire Pedigree Shires'. Where the main track swings to the right, go left onto a finger-posted track with large bungalow to your left. Passing stables and storage sheds to your left, the main track swings left but we go straight on here, beside an electricity post with junction box, to cross a narrow neck of field to a stile at the far side. Cross and continue forward with hedgeline to your left to a further stile. Cross this (not the stile in the corner of the field which leads off to the left) and continue up a narrow alley between garden fences and playing fields. Pass through a wicket gate and continue forward on a surfaced lane with brick wall to your left to arrive on Everton High Street. Go right, passing Brewery Lane to your left then go left onto Church Street and so to the magnificent church of Holy Trinity.

Everton was spelt 'Evretone' in Domesday Book and means 'the farmstead where wild boars are seen' – fortunately there are none to be found on the paths today!

It is a pleasant little village, with an old malthouse, threshing barn and brewery although, apart from the church, nothing predates the 16th century. Holy Trinity is a magnificent find! It is a church of battlements, which adorn the tower, clerestory and aisles with only the south porch boasting unobtrusive pinnacles. Externally, most of what we see is of the Perpendicular period but the bottom stages of the tower are Norman. Unfortunately, the tower was virtually ruined during a restoration in cement (!) in 1953 to mark the coronation of Queen Elizabeth II. There is a small pebble-dashed five-sided sanctuary built in 1841 and tucked away low down in the south wall of the nave, is some fine herringbone work. Above the south doorway is a beautifully carved early Norman (but with almost certain Viking influence) tympanum showing two horses licking each other's faces. Inside the church are magnificent Norman arches to the tower and chancel, and a beautiful round-topped west window. The tub font is an 1890 copy of the Norman original, the remains of which lie forlornly behind it, having been rescued from its life as a flowerpot in the vicarage garden. There are some fine internal monuments including one to 'Anthony Nevill of Grove, Major for King Charles the 1st and King Charles 2nd in the late rebellion who departed this life the 24th Feb 1688 aged 69, 9 months and odd days' and, hidden away beneath the tower, a worn coffin lid with a carving of a 13th-century knight and his lady. There is a list of vicars going back to Roger de Wengham (1280 to 1281) and an amusing list of 'Hints to those who worship God in this church' of which the first four are − 1. Be in time. 2. Go straight into church. 3. Kneel down on your knees. 4. Do not look round every time the door opens.

3. Leave the church by the south gate and go right along Church Street then bear left (not sharp left) down Ferry Lane, passing the Blacksmiths Arms to your left. At the T-junction (with Chapel Lane), go right and follow the lane as it bends left to become Harwell Lane. At the next T-junction, go right through the hamlet of Harwell, passing Nutcroft Way to your left. Just beyond the end of the red brick farm buildings to your right, go left up a stony track (Pinfold Lane) signed to Barrow Hills. At the top of the slope, where the main track swings to the left, go straight on, through a kissing gate to enter the beautiful wooded mound. Our path continues to the top of the slope where, at a major track crossing, we bear left to follow the contour ridge. Ignore tracks to the right and continue forward to a cross-track. Go straight on here into an area of broad-leaf trees, dropping gently then more steeply as the path bends to the left and meets a track at the bottom of the slope. Go left along the track with, initially, woodland up to the left and with views of Bawtry in the distance. Reaching a stony lane, go left to the A631 then turn left again along the roadside.

4. For the next half mile or so we keep to the pavement of the busy Bawtry − Gainsborough Road. This section cannot be described as the most pleasant of walks, however, it takes little more than ten minutes of undulation before we cross the road with care to go right onto an access track signed to Stone Hill Farm. The track dips then climbs gently. Just before the top of the slope, where the track bears to the right, go left beside a telegraph post onto a green lane (Youldholes Lane). We stay with this lane for about three-quarters of a mile, ignoring the (often indistinct) track (Stone Hill Lane) to the left. Eventually, at the end of a section with a low embankment up to the left and where the main track bears to the right, go left, up-slope, passing beneath power cables. At the top of the rise, go right along another green lane and continue to Mattersey Road.

5. Go right, using the surfaced walkway set in the grass verge and passing Everton Mill over to your left. Stay with the pathway, which meanders away from the road and drops gently. Pass the entrance to the water pumping station over the road to your left and, immediately beyond the adjacent cottage, where the footway approaches the road edge, go left, crossing the road and walking into a short section of surfaced driveway which is gated at its end. Take the finger-posted pathway, which crosses a stile to your right at the side of this drive, and bear left over a grassy area to enter a patch of woodland. Follow the pathway through the trees to emerge onto Eel Pool Road. Bear left over the road to pick up the track which we used to leave Mattersey at the beginning of our walk and which takes us over the River Idle and back to our start point.

6. Drakeholes – Gringley On The Hill – Clayworth – Wiseton

Distance: 9 miles (14.5km)

Maps: OS Landranger: 112 Scunthorpe. OS Explorer 280: Isle of Axholme; Scunthorpe & Gainsborough

Start: Drakeholes (GR 707903). Limited parking on the roadside verge, Drakeholes picnic area. Note: This is a popular spot and parking space can be quickly filled at weekends and holidays. Alternative start points may be found on the verge beside the Chesterfield Canal south of Wiseton or along roadside verges towards the eastern end of Church Lane, Clayworth.

Churches: St Peter and St Paul, Gringley; St Peter, Clayworth

The Walk

A lovely stretch of the Chesterfield Canal and a stroll along country lanes lead us to the beautifully sited church at Gringley on the Hill and the fine village viewpoints. We continue along green lanes and fieldpaths to Clayworth where we rejoin the canal for a walk back along the towpath to our start point.

Between Retford and Drakeholes the Chesterfield Canal is almost parallel to the River Idle but here, the river makes a great swing westwards before looping back to the east for its run to the Trent. In order to shorten the canal route, the Drakeholes tunnel was constructed to take it beneath the Bawtry to Gainsborough road, after which, staying with the relatively high ground, the canal would veer east, aiming more or less directly for its junction with the River Trent at West Stockwith. Twenty weeks were allowed for completion of the tunnel with a £1 penalty for each week that the work went over time. When completed (without penalty), the tunnel was 154m long and 4.7m (15ft 6 inches) high with the towpath having to go over the top of Cuckoo Hill. At the southern start of the tunnel a small basin and wharf were built, now a pleasant picnic spot, and it is here that we begin today's walk.

The Route

1. Leave the picnic area and follow the road up-slope, signed to Bawtry and Everton with The White Swan inn to your left and the picnic site to the right. [Note: do not be tempted to take a short-cut through the picnic area

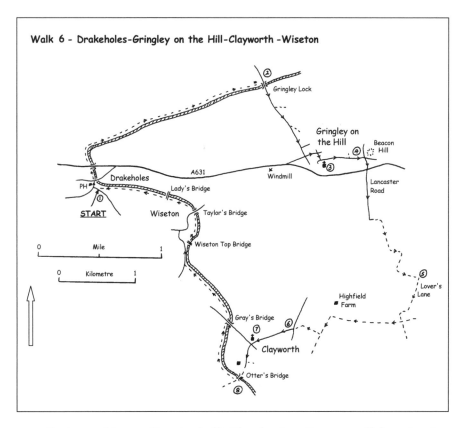

Walk 6 - Drakeholes-Gringley on the Hill-Clayworth -Wiseton

– the top end is usually wired off]. The short section we walk here is actually above the Drakeholes Tunnel (given the bridge number 73). At the top of the slope, bear right with the road, signed to Gainsborough and Gringley, for a few metres then, crossing the road with great care, go left up a stony track with a white house over a wall to your right. Keep the hedge to your left, ignoring a track leading to the right, and drop gently to join the canal towpath. We now continue with the canal to our right for nearly 1¾ miles as it runs initially northwards, passing beneath the busy A631 Gainsborough to Bawtry road (Bridge No 73A) then, soon, swinging sharply to the east. (The River Idle flows some three miles north of the canal here and much of the low lying land to our left was once useless marshland. Now its is heavily cultivated, the result of work by the Dutch engineer Sir Cornelius Vermuyden who was called in by Charles II in the 17th century to drain this and other areas of eastern England). There are fine views out over the flatlands to the left and no bridges to dip under until we arrive at Gringley Lock (Bridge No 74).

2. Leave the canal here, climbing the embankment to the road and going right to pass over the waterway. Continue up the gentle incline towards the village of Gringley on the Hill, ignoring finger-posted footpaths to the left. Soon, the pinnacled church tower appears on the ridge ahead and, to the right, the old mill tower. Go forward into the outskirts of the village, passing Laycock Avenue to your left and at the crossroads ahead go left onto West Wells Lane. At the next cross-roads, with Methodist chapels on the corner ahead and to the left, follow the road as it bears right (as Crosshill), still climbing gently to the market cross. (This has been lovingly restored with funds raised locally to celebrate the Millennium. A plaque tells us that the village was granted a market charter on 2nd November, 1252 although, as with many such markets, activities had ceased by the 16th century). At the junction with High Street, go left to the gateway and steps to the church.

The village name appears as 'Gringeleia' in Domesday Book, the origin being Old English with the possible meaning of 'the woodland clearing of the people living at the green place'. Gringley occupies a beautiful ridge-top site 82ft (25m) above sea level. Perhaps not a mountain, but in an area of flat, low-lying land, a great spot to survey the surrounding countryside of Nottinghamshire, Lincolnshire and Yorkshire. Many of the older houses and farms are built of local brick and to the west of the village is the tower of a four-storey windmill, dating from 1830. The church of St Peter and St Paul is beautifully sited and is a real mixture of styles. Much of the structure belongs to the Perpendicular period, most noticeably the clerestory and the upper stages of the tower – typical of this part of Nottinghamshire however, the north arcade is Early English. There is a south and a west doorway but the two northern ones are especially interesting since they span the period from Norman (the blocked doorway in the north wall of the tower) to classical 17th century (in the north aisle). These doors would indicate perhaps the age of the lower stages of the tower and of a 17th-century rebuild of the large north aisle incorporating a contemporary doorway. An old stone coffin leans against the tower beside the Norman doorway. The church was in a state of ruin at the beginning of the last century but a major and successful rebuild was undertaken which included the addition of a tasteful south aisle.

3. Back on High Street, go right, passing the Blue Bell inn to your left and continue to the junction with Green Road/Beacon Hill Road. Our route goes right here, but a short diversion to climb Beacon Hill is well worth the effort. So, cross diagonally left over the junction, mount some steps and pass through a gateway then up the grassy slope to the top of the viewpoint. This is the highest point for miles around and is a bit of a mystery. It looks as though it must have been an ancient hill fort but excavations have revealed nothing to confirm this. It is also said to have

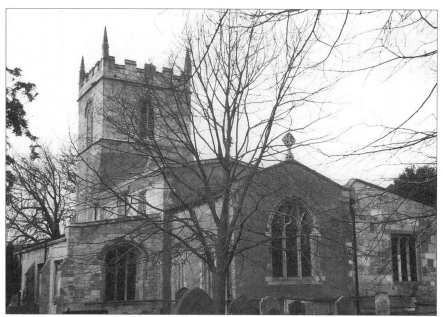

St Peter and St Paul, Gringley

been an encampment where Prince Rupert rested before riding to the relief of Newark during the Civil War.

4. Return through the gateway and the steps to go left, down Green Road, to the busy A631. Cross the dual carriageway with the greatest of care and continue down Lancaster Road, the narrow surfaced lane opposite. The lane slowly deteriorates as it drives southwards then westwards before a right turn takes us south again. We are now on the Trent Valley Way and walking a magnificent ridge with views left, towards Lincolnshire and the Trent valley power stations, and an endless panorama to the right. This is very much a zigzag track and for much of the way we can see Clayworth church, our next port of call, which at times is tantalisingly ahead, or sometimes to our rear. Staying with the main track, we eventually emerge into a field corner. Go forward here along the headland with the hedge to your right for a few metres then right, still with the headland and hedge right. At the field corner, go left with the headland, to arrive eventually at a line of trees and bushes stretching off to the right.

5. Go right here, over a finger-posted and waymarked (Trent Valley Way) plank bridge and into the trees to follow a well-defined and sinuous pathway known as Lover's Lane. Emerging from the trees, go right along

a short section of green lane then bear left, beside a stile, onto a headland path. Keep the hedge to your left for about 100m and at a waymarked cross-track, go right, (leaving the Trent Valley Way which goes forward) down the centre of the huge field and along what is, in most seasons of the year, a well-defined bridleway. At the field edge, continue through a lovely avenue of bushes and trees to pick up a headland track with a hedge to your right. Cross the farm track at the field corner and go forward through a fieldgate and onto another section of green lane. Soon we pass through a bridlegate and continue over a narrow neck of grazing land, through a farm gate and out onto a track with Highfield Farm up to the right. Go left here through a finger-posted bridlegate and onto another green lane with bushes, hedges and trees to either side. This is Toft Dyke Lane, which continues all the way to Wheatley Road south of Clayworth, but we need to turn off to the right 300m down it. Our path is waymarked over a culvert and stile and into a field corner. Follow the headland with the hedgeline to your left to cross a stile in the field corner; then, continue along a short section of green lane onto Gringley Road (the B1403).

6.   Cross the road with care and continue down Church Lane to enter the village of Clayworth. Pass the cemetery guarded by a lych gate to the right and there before us is the church of St Peter.

Clayworth lies astride the Roman Road which linked Lincoln to York via Doncaster. The road itself crossed the Trent at Littleborough (Segelocum) and then continued through Sturton le Steeple and Wheatley to arrive here. More recently, Clayworth was the home of the Otter family who arrived in the 16th century and established themselves at Royston Manor (the remains of which we shall soon pass). The village name was spelt 'Clauworde' in Domesday Book and comes from the Old English meaning 'the enclosure on the low curving hill'. The church of St Peter is a large building and although the tower has that typical Nottinghamshire Perpendicular look, the lower stages are much older – probably Saxon or early Norman. The nave has some 13th-century arches with Norman bases to the pillars although the main structure and the clerestory above it are 15th century. The chancel is Early English and there is a fine 13th-century chancel arch but sections of the wall between it and the nave have herringbone masonry indicating more Norman/Saxon work. Between the nave and the chancel is a fine screen, the base dating from pre-Reformation times while, in the south wall of the chancel, a 13th-century archway leads into the Chapel of St Nicholas. Between this chapel and the south aisle is a simple stone screen dating from 1388. There was a major restoration in 1874, which included the south porch although the door within is probably Norman, as is the inner north door. Over the entrance to the porch is a sundial with the inscription – *Our days on the earth are as a* shadow. The church has two fonts – one Medieval, the other probably dating from the 17th century. The church abounds with memorials, many in brass and dating from the 16th, 17th and 18th centuries. There are some fine examples to the Acklom family, early owners of Wiseton, whose members distinguished themselves at the siege of Scarborough Castle during the Civil War, and to the Otters of nearby Royston Manor. The oldest memorial is a worn floorstone beneath the tower to a Rector of 1448. Also in the tower is a memorial to William Sampson, another Rector, who founded the first village school and who left behind a history of the parish for the years 1676 to 1701. In the chancel is the Tudor tomb to Judge Humphrey Fitzwilliam who died in 1559 and his wife. There is so much to see here, but do not leave before noting the list of Rectors going back to Robert de Clayworth in 1226.

7. Leave the church by the south gateway and go straight over Town Street/Wiseton Road to continue down St Peter's Lane, soon passing the modern driveway of Royston Manor, previously the home of the Otter family to your right. There is nothing to be seen of the original Elizabethan building and the 1891 rebuild has been turned into a modern country club and hotel complex. Ignore finger-posted pathways to the left and continue on the main track as it drops to the Chesterfield Canal at Otter's Bridge (No 68).

8. Cross the bridge and go right along the towpath with the waterway to your right and with views of Royston Hall and of the church over. We pass beneath a road bridge (No 69) and continue all the way to a lane which parallels the canal just south of Wiseton. Continue with the lane but where it swings left into the hamlet, bear right, staying with the canal bank and passing beneath Wiseton Top Bridge (No 70). Once around the canal bend, we get fine views of Gringley far over to the right while, over the hedgeline to the left, is the hamlet of Wiseton. (This is an attractive little place, which was originally the home of the Acklom family. The Estate and Hall passed to the Laycocks in the 19th century but the family died out, the last being General 'Lucky' Laycock who was Governor of Malta during the Second World War. The Hall, dating from 1771 was pulled down in 1960 but there are still a couple of ancillary buildings remaining including the rather fine laundry with its tall chimney pots and line of dormer windows which can be seen from our path). The next bridge (Taylor's Bridge, No 71) marks the northern edge of the hamlet and our route leads us through the old Acklom estate to yet another little bridge known as Lady's Bridge which has bearded faces mounted in the centre of its arches. A little over half-a-mile of fine towpath walking brings us back to our start point.

7. Walkeringham – West Stockwith – Misterton

Distance: 8½ miles (13.5km)

Maps: OS Landranger 112: Scunthorpe. OS Explorer 280: Isle of Axholme; Scunthorpe & Gainsborough

Start: Walkeringham Nature Reserve Car Park (GR 755926).

Churches: St Mary Magdalen, Walkeringham; St Mary, West Stockwith; All Saints, Misterton

The Walk

A stroll in the flatlands of north-east Nottinghamshire following sections of all three major water features of our area – the Rivers Trent and Idle and the Chesterfield Canal. We take in the very start/end of both the Trent Valley Way and the Cuckoo Way and visit three churches of totally different styles.

Our walk begins at the Nottinghamshire Wildlife Trust reserve on the outskirts of Walkeringham. The village itself is cut into two distinct parts by The Moor, with the main centre of population and church being to the east. In Domesday Book, Walkeringham appears as 'Wacheringeham', meaning 'the homestead of the followers (or family) of Walhhere', the personal name being of Old English origin.

The Route

1. Return to the B1403 and go right, then take the first right onto Caves Lane (there is a slight variation in spelling on the name-plates at either end) which leads into the western part of Walkeringham. At the T-junction with the Brickmaker's Arms down to your left, go right along North Moor Road then right again onto West Moor Road, the village church now becoming visible over fields to the front left. Where the road bends left as South Moor Road, go forward along a track and, where this swings to the right, go forward onto a finger-posted headland path with hedgeline to your right. Pass through a wide gap at the field corner and continue between fields to a stile onto a road.

2. Go left along this pleasant meandering highway passing Mill Lane to your right then Brickenhole Lane left and continue down into the village to find the gateway and steps to the church.

St Mary Magdalen, Walkeringham

St Mary Magdalen is a typical North Nottinghamshire Perpendicular-style building with ashlar-faced, battlemented tower sporting corner and intervening crocketed pinnacles. There is an abundance of battlements on the north and south aisles and clerestory, although the chancel and south porch (beside which lies an ancient and broken stone coffin), are undecorated. There are fine east and west windows and, inside, there is a plain octagonal font with the inscription 'RC 1663'. The glory of the church though is a magnificent monument to Francis Williamson and his wife, the former dying in 1639. This contains the fascinating epitaph – 'My life to lose, my soul to save, My goods to spend, I took, I gave, See what remains all you that pass, And make my monument your glass. Mistake not youth nor ladies fair, A glass but not to curl your hair. No flatterer; but true and just, it measures out your time in dust. All men do ere and judge amiss, 'til they have viewed themselves in this, which to the reader shows thus much, some few hours past and thou art such. Then thoughts and cares for long life save, and be undressing for the grave.' The nave arcades and the arcade to the north chancel chapel – the oldest parts of the church – date from the 13th century and a clue to the age of the original building is best obtained from the list of vicars which goes back to Henri de Raeti in 1237.

3. Leave the church by the little wooden lych gate with its flat roof and castle turrets at the north-west corner of the churchyard and go forward along Gringley Road. At the A161 junction with the base of the old market cross to your right, go left, signed to Goole and Misterton. With the Fox and Hounds inn to your left, go right onto Station Road. Stay with the road as it runs out of the village then passes over a railway crossing to become Marsh Road. Pass Holmes Lane to your right and where the lane bends sharply to the left, go forward through a gateway and onto the Trent bank.

4. Walk left along the embankment for a mile or so, keeping the Trent to your right, the distant spire of Misterton church soon coming into view to the front left. Our path eventually joins a road on the outskirts of West Stockwith and we continue along the pavement with a wall separating us from the river to the right. 150m on, where the road bends to the left, bear right down a finger-posted lane with the river still over a wall to the right. Cross the magnificent Stockwith Lock (the start/end of the Cuckoo Way where the Chesterfield Canal flows into the Trent), and continue along the grass embankment with the little church at East Stockwith in Lincolnshire over the river to your right. Where the embankment joins a wall, drop down steps onto the road. Go right along the road, crossing the bridge over the River Idle and on to the church of St Mary, West Stockwith (the start/end of the Trent Valley Way).

West Stockwith marks the point where the River Idle, the Mother Drain and Chesterfield Canal join the River Trent. Today it is a little gem hidden in the north-east corner of the county but, in the 17th and 18th centuries, its waterway accesses made it an important inland port with thriving boatyards and warehouses. The Trent separates it from its neighbour in Lincolnshire and today there is no physical connection between the two. The earliest mention of the settlement is in the 12th century when it was spelt 'Stochithe', coming from the Old English meaning 'the landing place made of logs and tree stumps'. The church of St Mary is a solid Georgian structure comprising a red brick rectangular box topped by a white wooden cupola. It was built in 1722 (the date can be seen above the west doorway) with funds left by William Huntingdon, a ship's carpenter, whose tomb is inside the church. The church was restored in 1963 but an indication of a much older structure is given by the attractive and tiny octagonal font on a pedestal and used as a flower pot in the garden between the church and the Trent.

5. Walk back over the River Idle bridge, ignoring the finger-posted path signed to Haxey Gate. On the far side of the river, go right onto a short section of surfaced lane, with the river to your right. Continue forward along the grassy embankment, eventually walking a causeway with the Idle to your right and the Mother Drain to the left. Just beyond the beautifully converted pumping station with its two brick towers, go left, leaving the river, and follow a lane signed 'Public Footpath to Misterton – 1'. Ignore finger-posted footpaths to the right and continue along the mean-

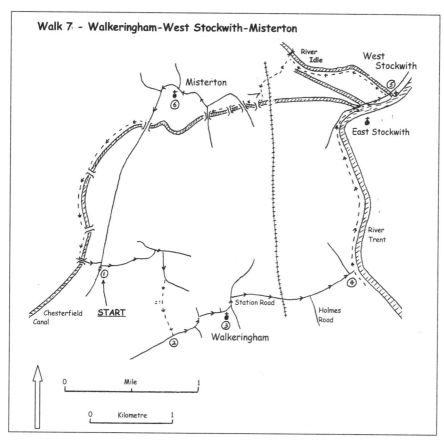

Walk 7 - Walkeringham-West Stockwith-Misterton

dering lane, which takes us beneath the railway bridge and into the outskirts of Misterton. At the road junction, go forward then bear left, with the entrance to The Packet Inn car park then the wooden fence of an electricity sub station immediately to your left and join the Chesterfield Canal towpath. Go right, under Bridge No 83 and, passing Misterton Low Lock, continue under the road bridge (No 82A). Keeping the canal to your left, pass Misterton Top Lock and duck beneath Bridge No 82. Just before the next bridge (No 81), bear right beside a power post to emerge onto a road and the outskirts of Misterton. Go right along the road and at a T-junction, go left to pass a number of interesting buildings including: the Victoria Institute (erected in 1897 to celebrate 60 years of Queen Victoria's reign); the Board Schools (1872); the Temperance Hall (also 1872) and the impressive Methodist Hall and Chapel, (1878), eventually reaching the church.

Misterton is spelt 'Ministretone' in Domesday Book and comes from the Old English meaning 'estate with a church belonging to a monastery'. The village owes much of its prosperity to King Charles I who appointed Sir Cornelius Vermuyden, a Dutch engineer, to drain the surrounding marshes. The reclaimed area provided excellent arable land and so the village flourished. In 1777 the Chesterfield Canal was opened, linking the village to other towns in the county and the clay cut from the canal was found to be ideal for making bricks — thousands of which were needed to build the canal locks and bridges. This resulted in many local brickworks being established. The remains of several of these can still be seen nearby. All Saints is a rarity in North Nottinghamshire — a church with a broach spire which rises to a height of 100ft, dates from the 13th century and was meticulously rebuilt in 1847 after being struck by lightning. Again, unlike many of the churches in the area it is quite plain — no pinnacles, no crockets and no battlements. The south doorway is 12th century although the door itself is of the period 1800-1850. Inside there is a fine arch dating from the 13th century which links the tower to the nave and a magnificent sealed archway of the same period which would have led to a north aisle extension. The north arcade comes from the 14th century, while that to the south is a hundred years later. Much of the remainder of the building, including the clerestory, is 15th century. The base of the font dates from the 13th century, whilst the bowl is of 1662. There is a large hatchment above the chancel arch, dated 1721 and the church is full of interesting memorials. One of these, in the north aisle, is to Charles Grayburn, commander of the brig *Charles of Gainsbro* who was lost with the whole of his crew in the British Channel during a heavy storm in 1824 and also to his great, great grandson, Sub Lieut Charles William Grayburn Richardson, RNVR, who was killed in action operating from the aircraft carrier HMS *Nairana* in 1944. Also well worth finding is a list of vicars going back to Roger de O'yley in 1254.

6. Leave the church by the east gate and go left then left again onto the B1403, passing the Red Hart inn over the road to your right. After about 700 meandering metres and immediately before crossing the Chesterfield Canal, go right, down steps to the canal bank. The bridge here is No 80 and we now join the Trent Valley Way. Continue along the towpath with the canal to your left, passing beneath Bridge No 79 where the church tower at Gringley on the Hill becomes visible on the distant horizon, then Bridge 78. At the next, Bridge No 77, where the main span has been replaced with concrete, climb up the embankment and go left, over the canal, and follow the lane (Brickyard Lane) to the B1403. Turn right along the road, (taking care since verges are minimal), passing Cave's Lane to your left and so back to the start point.

8. Hayton – North Wheatley – South Wheatley – Clarborough

Distance: 8 miles (13km)

Maps: OS Landranger 120: Mansfield & Worksop, Sherwood Forest. OS Explorer 271: Newark-on-Trent; Retford, Southwell & Saxilby

Start: St Peter's church, Hayton (GR 727842). Grass verge parking on Church Lane close to the church. Please park 'prettily'.

Churches: St Peter, Hayton; St Peter and St Paul, North Wheatley; St Helen, South Wheatley; St John the Baptist, Clarborough

The Walk

Leaving the church at Hayton, a short section of canal walking takes us along green lanes and fieldpaths to the Wheatley villages which boast two churches, one of them a wonderful romantic ruin. More green lanes lead us to Clarborough where we rejoin the Chesterfield Canal and the towpath back to our start point.

We start our walk at the western edge of the village of Hayton which is not mentioned in Domesday Book but appears as 'Heiton' in 1175, the name coming from the Old English meaning the 'farmstead where hay is made or stored'. The village itself almost runs into Clarborough as it hugs the narrow corridor between the Wheatley Hills and the Chesterfield Canal, but the church of St Peter lives in a world of its own, standing alone outside the village and close to the canal. The church is quite plain, having a spindly west tower with battlements and gargoyles, nave, chancel, battlemented south aisle and a south porch. Only the porch has pinnacles and these are ornamented with fine crockets, the bottom ones carved as weird human and animal faces. The south doorway dates from the 12th century, as does the south arcade, but much of the remainder of the building, including the tower and the octagonal font with (recently carved) decorated panels are of the 14th century.

The Route

1. Go left out of the church gate and walk down the lane to cross the canal (Bridge No 63). Drop down right to the towpath and keeping the canal to your right, pass beneath bridges 64, 65 and, immediately after Bridge 66 go sharply left and climb up onto the road. Go left, crossing the waterway

with The Boat Inn to your right. The main road swings sharply right here but we go left along Burntleys Road and follow it as it bends right to climb gently away from the canal. At the brow of the initial slope with surfaced lanes going left and right, go forward onto an earth and stone track, still climbing gently along what is now a wonderful green lane with increasingly magnificent views.

2. At the slope-top T-junction, go right, down-slope, for a few metres, then left over a waymarked stile beside fieldgate. Continue along the top of the field, with a hedge left, to cross a stile at the field corner. [Note: This field is sometimes divided by temporary gates/fences]. Ignore the track dropping down to the right and go forward over the field, aiming for the left-hand cooling tower of West Burton Power Station, which can be seen in the distance ahead. The path drops gently to an embankment at the far side of the field where we go left, along the embankment top. At the field corner, go right, down the slope, to pick up a path that eventually follows a hedgeline to your left. At the far hedge, go left, keeping the hedge to your right (the definitive line is on the far side of the hedge but we follow the walked route), climbing gently to a farm track. Go right here, passing farm buildings to your right and continue for half a mile to the Retford Road.

3. Cross the dual-carriageway with care then bear left, down the slope of a slip road to enter the village of North Wheatley. At Low Street, with The Sun Inn on the corner to your right, cross, and continue along Top Street, which becomes Middlefield Road and leads to the church.

    Wheatley comprises two distinct settlements, separated today by just a couple of fields. In Domesday Book, the area is referred to as 'Wateleie', coming from the Old English meaning 'the clearing where wheat is grown' – not much has changed – although nowadays, the area is most famous for its strawberries. Apart from the stumpy battlemented 15th century tower, the church of St Peter and St Paul at North Wheatley is an uncluttered building, lacking further crenellations, pinnacles and crockets. The whole is a very plain ashlared structure of nave and chancel. There are no aisles, but there is a fine, half-timbered south porch and an unusual squared-off sealed doorway in the north wall of the nave. Inside, there is a Norman font and there are some fine memorials of the 15th century. The chancel was heavily restored in 1825 and further restoration work was completed in 1896.

4. Leave the church by the west gate and go left, dropping down (Church Hill). (At the bottom of the slope to the right is the Old Hall which carries the arms of the Cartwright family and the date 1673 above the door). Go left into Low Pasture Lane, passing a footbridge to your right, which

St Peter and St Paul, North Wheatley

leads to playing fields at the rear of the school. After another100m, go right, crossing another footbridge then left, with tennis courts to your right and beck to the left. Cross a stile into a meadow and walk up-slope aiming slightly to the right of the tower of the ruined church that can be seen ahead. At the top of the field, climb the stile and continue along a narrow alley with the church left and garden hedge/fence right, to emerge onto Sturton Road. The gateway into the churchyard is to your left.

St Helen is a beautifully located romantic ruin set amongst trees. All that remains today is a 15th-century unadorned tower, filled with the cooing of doves, a sealed tower arch and a tiny Norman chancel arch – all overgrown with ivy and elder. The building was pulled down by the Victorian vandals and was a ruin by 1883, its chalice and altar table passing to the church at North Wheatley and the font found its way to a church in Nottingham. This must though have been a very small building since the distance between chancel and tower arches is no more than 25ft! In the churchyard, which is still in use, can be found the remains of crocketed pinnacles which once must have graced this little building.

5. Return to Sturton Road and go right, soon passing the entrance to the Village Hall and car park to your right. Where the road bends sharply to the right, go left along the finger-posted Muspit(s) Lane. This surfaced lane, part of the Trent Valley Way, quickly becomes a dirt track as it climbs gently, leaving farm buildings and houses behind. Ignore finger-posted paths to the left and continue forward along this magnificent ridgeway as it drives south-westwards, eventually dropping with a

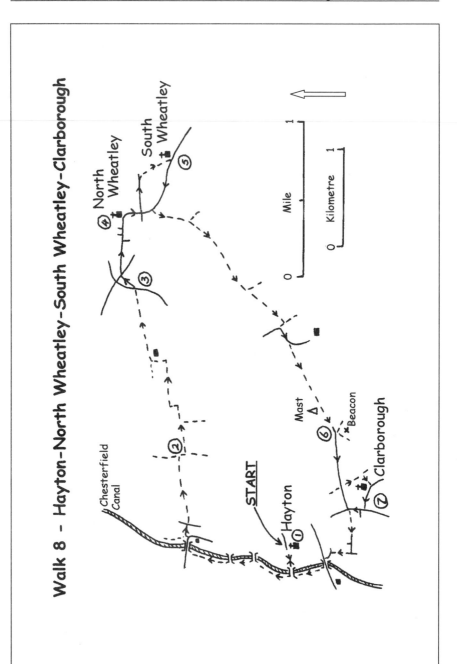

Walk 8 – Hayton-North Wheatley-South Wheatley-Clarborough

hedge to your right and arriving at a cross-track. Go right for 100m then left along what is now a surfaced lane. The lane climbs gently to swing left towards farm buildings and here, go forward on a hard earth track with communications mast ahead. Pass the mast and continue gently down to a track junction with the Clarborough village beacon over to your left.

6. Bear right, dropping on a surfaced lane with magnificent views ahead including, to the front-right, distant Hayton church tower. Immediately before the first houses of Clarborough, go left, onto a finger-posted foot-path and into an area of scrub and trees. Continue to cross a stile into the bottom of a field where the tower of Clarborough church finally becomes visible ahead then go forward over two more stiles and enter the north-east corner of the church. Bear right, down steps, to follow the path to the south porch.

Clarborough hugs a fine site with the Wheatley Hills rising to the east and the Chesterfield Canal to the west. It is given as 'Claureburg' in Domesday Book, which comes from the Old English meaning the 'old fortification overgrown with clover'. To what this refers is not known but maybe, beneath local fields, there are ancient defence works still to be uncovered? St John the Baptist is a typical North Nottinghamshire church of battlemented tower with corner crocketed pinnacles, nave, chancel, aisles and south porch. The north arcade dates from the 13th century while most of the remainder of the building is of the Perpendicular period. Externally this is still a fine church but the inside shows the heavy restoration of 1874.

7. Leave the church by the lych gate beyond the tower and go right along Church Lane. At the main road, go right again, passing Big Lane to your left then go left down Little Lane, a surfaced path between trees, bushes and garden fences, to emerge onto the end of a cul-de-sac (South View Drive) in a residential estate. Go forward to a T-junction, then right, along a road that quickly ends at a field edge. Bear right on a well-walked field path which runs parallel to power posts to your right to arrive on Celery Meadows Road. Go left, crossing a bridge then immediately left again along Gill Green Walk, a surfaced path which runs along the front of houses and keeps bending to the right, eventually joining Smeath Lane. Go left along the road, crossing the Chesterfield Canal (beware of traffic on the bridge) then drop down right to the towpath at Bridge No 62. (The Gate Inn is 100m down the road here should you require refreshment!) Follow the towpath with the canal to your right and with views of Hayton church tower to the front right. At the next bridge (No 63), climb up onto Church Lane and continue back to the start point.

9. Sturton le Steeple – Clarborough Nature Reserve – North Leverton

Distance: 7½ miles (12km)

Maps: OS Landranger 120: Mansfield & Worksop, Sherwood Forest. OS Explorer 271: Newark-on-Trent; Retford, Southwell & Saxilby

Start: St Peter and St Paul, Church Street, Sturton le Steeple (GR 788839). Limited parking on the grass verge east of the church and school. Note that during term time, the surfaced layby outside the school is for the use of the staff.

Churches: St Peter and St Paul, Sturton le Steeple; St Martin, North Leverton

The Walk

A stroll along green lanes with wide views and visits to two lovely churches, a hidden nature reserve and to the only working windmill left in Nottinghamshire. Much of our route will follow the Trent Valley Way and we return to our start point from North Leverton along a cross-field section of this long distance pathway.

Sturton le Steeple is an attractive little village grouped around its church and pub. It lies on the old Roman road which linked Lincoln with Doncaster and which crossed the River Trent at Littleborough to the east. The name is spelt 'Estretone' in Domesday Book which describes its position as 'the town on the street' – referring to the old Roman road. The suffix 'steeple' appears in the 18th century and refers to the steeple-like pinnacles on the church tower. Our walk begins at this birthday-cake church of St Peter and St Paul, a landmark for miles around with its ashlar-faced and battlemented tower capped with no less than twelve crocketed pinnacles. The 14th-century tower is all that remains of the original building which was burnt down in 1901 but, happily, the rebuilt sections retain their Medieval look. Just surviving is a Norman window and doorway in the north chancel wall and the Norman doorway of the south porch. The bowl of the font is also Norman, having come from the vanished church of West Burton; tucked away in the darkness beneath the tower are a number of large Georgian monuments which were rescued from the fire. These include one to the widow of Sir Richard Earl of Stragglethorpe in Lincolnshire who died in 1687. Here also is a very worn effigy of a lady dating from the 13th century. There is a painting of the Mayflower, commemorating the 350th anniversary of its sailing to America. Specifically, it remembers John Robinson, who was pastor of the Pilgrim Fathers and Bridget, his wife, who were born in Sturton. Also, John Calver who married Bridget's sister and became the first Governor of the New England colony.

The Route

1. Leaving the church grounds, go left along Church Street, passing the Reindeer Inn to your right and go straight over Cross Street/Leverton Road to enter Springs Lane and join the Trent Valley Way. We follow this lovely lane, its surface deteriorating to an earth and stone track, for about a mile then bear right and pass beneath the railway arch and onto what is now High House Road. Our route mounts very gently now for about a mile and a quarter to achieve an eventual height of 67m. Along the way, we have distant views to the right of North Wheatley church and a magnificent panorama over the Trent Valley behind us.

2. Go left with the track as it swings towards Sturton High House (farm), then almost immediately right, through a hedge gap and bridlegate, to pick up a headland path with a hedge to your right and sight of the huge radio mast above Clarborough in the distance ahead. Pass through another bridlegate and continue with the headland to a gap at the bottom field corner and onto a muddy track crossing the front. Go left along what is known as Blue Stocking Lane, (the Trent Valley Way goes off to the right here) climbing and meandering gently and, ignoring all side tracks, eventually emerge onto a surfaced lane. Go left towards the farmhouse for 200m then right, down a finger-posted bridleway (Rathole Lane) which we follow to the railway crossing at the bottom of the valley. (Our route continues forward over the railway but a slight diversion into the Nature Reserve here makes a good break). Immediately before the railway line then, go right over a stile and cross the meadow with the railway line to your left and so into Clarborough Nature Reserve. (Also called Rathole Nature Reserve, this delightfully hidden spot occupies the railway cutting edge and roof of the railway tunnel of the Retford to Gainsborough line. It covers an area of about 15 acres and has been left virtually undisturbed since the building of the railway in 1849. It is a densely wooded area now noted for its orchids and butterflies).

3. Return to Rathole Lane and go right, taking care crossing the railway line then begin the gentle climb up what is now Caddow Lane, soon with woodland to the left and then to the right. At the brow of the slope and close to a wooden power post, go left onto a wide green lane (Retford Gate). Ignore all side tracks and stay with the main lane with, initially,

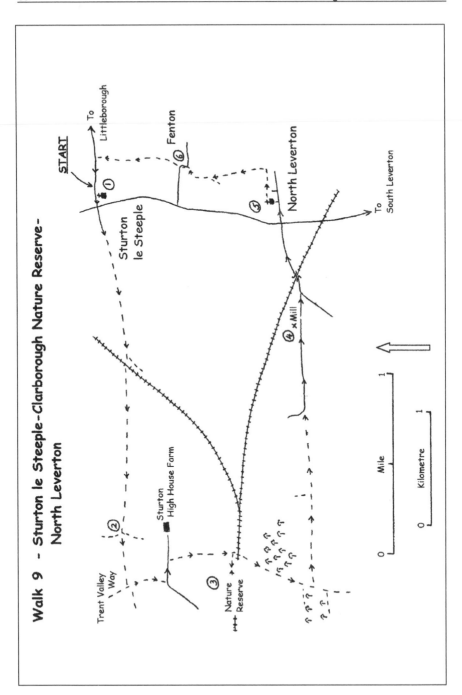

Walk 9 – Sturton le Steeple–Clarborough Nature Reserve– North Leverton

distant views of Cottam Power Station to the front-right then a massive panorama of the Trent Valley ahead. We remain with the lane for about a mile and a half as it undulates, mainly downwards, and improves to a surfaced lane as we approach North Leverton Windmill. (This beautiful four-sailed structure is the only working windmill in Nottinghamshire and is open to the public on Sunday afternoons. It was built by a consortium of local farmers in 1813 and at that time was lower than the present building so that the sails could be serviced from the ground. It was raised to it present height in 1884).

4. Continue to the Retford Road and bear left along the pavement, passing beneath the railway bridge and continuing into the pleasant village of North Leverton. Go straight over the village centre cross-roads with the Royal Oak Inn and then the school to your left to go left onto a finger-posted lane. This leads between house gardens and over a bridged beck into the grounds of St Martin.

North Leverton appears as 'Legretone' in Domesday Book and probably means the 'farmstead on a stream called Legre' — a Celtic name of uncertain meaning. The full name of the village today is 'North Leverton with Habblesthorpe', described in an edition of the Guinness Book of Records as the longest multiple place name in England. Habblesthorpe was once a parish in its own right but was

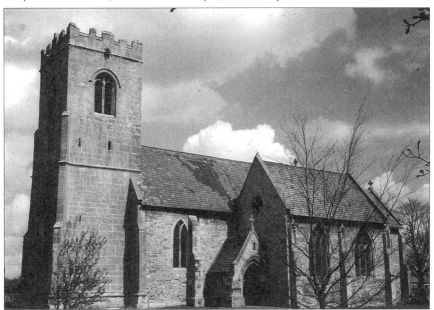

St Martin, North Leverton

combined with North Leverton in 1884. The church of St Martin has a slim, ashlar-faced Perpendicular tower with unadorned battlements but the remainder of the structure is of much older stonework. The whole feeling here is of slimness, the only addition to the narrow nave, chancel and south porch being a strange chapel-looking aisle attached to the south side of the building. This dates from the early 14th century. There is an empty niche above the south porch and the doorway inside dates from around 1200. There are fine east and west windows and a sealed late Norman doorway in the north wall of the nave.

5. Leave the church by the pathway and little gate to the north-east which leads onto a lane. Go right along the lane and, where it swings to the right, go straight on. The lane becomes a grassy path then a muddy track through thick bushes with, eventually, a beck down to the right. Just beyond a footbridge to your right, go left, over a stile, and follow the headland with hedge to your left. (We are now back on the Trent Valley Way). Cross the stile at the field corner then go left for a few metres then right, with the waymarker. Go over the field, aiming for the left-hand cooling tower of West Burton Power Station, which can be seen in the distance ahead. At the far side of the field, cross the plank and stile and continue over a narrow neck of meadow to another stile. Cross this and continue along the headland with a hedge to your right, crossing two more stiles then, eventually, a plank bridge and stile onto a field edge. Follow the diverted path signs here, which take us right, left then left again, around the headland, to a stile onto Fenton Lane.

6. Cross the lane and the stile on the far side to go forward then left, along the field edge with a thick line of trees and bushes to your right. Cross the stile at the field corner and continue along a headland path with ditch and hedgeline to your right. (Ahead, the horizon is dominated by the cooling towers of West Burton Power Station but, to the left, rises the lovely tower of Sturton le Steeple church). At the end of this very long field, cross the bridge and stile then go right then left, along the headland with hedge then trees right to cross the stile in a 'false' field corner, then forward to a stile onto Low Holland Lane. Go left to return to our start point.

10. South Leverton – Treswell – Rampton – Cottam

Distance: 9 miles (14.5km)

Maps: OS Landranger 121: Lincoln & Newark-on-Trent. OS Explorer 271: Newark-on-Trent; Retford, Southwell & Saxilby

Start: Village Hall, Town Street, South Leverton (GR 784810). Limited parking on the roadside car park opposite The Plough inn. [Note that parking on the north side of the road is for patrons of the inn]. If more than a couple of vehicles are to use this area, please check with the keyholder. Alternatively, park at the junction of Rampton Lane and Meadow Dike Lane (both green lanes which we use in our walk at GR 788808) but please pull onto the grass verges here since the lanes themselves are used by farm vehicles.

Churches: All Saints, South Leverton; St John the Baptist, Treswell; All Saints, Rampton; Holy Trinity, Cottam

---

The Walk

A wealth of fine and varied churches are visited on this walk which, in addition to green lanes and quiet country roads, includes a cross-field section which can be muddy when wet and which will not always be clearly visible when cropped or under the plough.

South Leverton is another attractive North Nottinghamshire village with pleasant pub and church and a Quaker Meeting House which was established in 1650. It is not certain which of the Levertons is mentioned in Domesday Book, which only has 'Legretone', probably meaning the 'farmstead on a stream called the Legre', a Celtic river name of uncertain meaning.

The Route

1. With your back to the Village Hall, go right along Town Street for a few metres with The Plough Inn over to your left and, immediately beyond the pub, go left up a narrow finger-posted alley which gently mounts and bends to the left to enter the east end of the churchyard.

   All Saints is a dream of a church with its magnificent slim and unbuttressed Norman tower of which only the 15th-century battlements and the clock installed to mark the Silver Jubilee of Queen Elizabeth II in 1977 are later additions. There was a fine Norman doorway in the west wall of the tower but this has been sealed and into it is cut a 13th-century window. The south doorway is a magnificent Norman example although the porch that protects it is much later. Internally, the nave has 13th-century arcades. While the south aisle has some fine 14th-century window tracery, the sealed doorway at the west end is a mystery; it may have led to a previous extension of the tower. The windows in the north aisle also date from the late 14th century. The Medieval chancel with its 13th-century windows was restored in 1868 and the remainder of the building was restored 30 years later.

Returning to Town Street, go left, and, ignoring finger-posted paths to left and right, continue to the crossing with Rampton Lane. Go right, up the lane, passing farm accesses to left and right to arrive at a cross-track (with Meadow Dike Lane – the alternative parking place).

2. Go forward along a hard earth and stony track for about half a mile with distant views of the cooling towers of Cottam Power Station over to the left and those at High Marnham ahead. Where the main route swings to the left, continue forward along a lesser track, with, to your right, Ashton's Meadow nature reserve. Pass a 'nodding donkey' enclosure to your right and continue along what is now a headland path with hedge to your right. Cross the stile in the field corner and stay with the headland to another stile and continue to a broken tree-line stretching off to the left. Go right here, over a stile, to pass through an overgrown green lane and join a farm track. Ignore the track left which leads to another 'nodding donkey' and the finger-posted footpath beyond, staying with the main track to arrive at a road. Go left along the roadside (take care – there are minimal verges) for about 300m to arrive at Treswell church.

St John the Baptist stands at the northern extremity of the village which appears as 'Tireswelle' in Domesday Book and comes from the Old English meaning 'the spring (or stream) of a man called Tir'. The church is a mainly 15th-century building of tall battlemented tower, nave, chancel, north aisle and south porch, although the chancel actually comes from the early 14th century and the south porch, although Perpendicular, hides a fine 13th-century doorway. Of greatest interest on the outside of the building is a beautifully carved Norman coffin lid set into the south wall of the chancel. Inside the church, a good octagonal font matches the shape of the piers supporting the bays for the Perpendicular north aisle. This is a lovely little place, the whole shaded by magnificent trees and set beside the tiny stream of Lea Beck.

3. Return to the road and go right to enter the village. At the T-junction, go left, signed to Cottam and Rampton. Pass The Red Lion inn (changing ownership at the time of writing thus it might be renamed or even shut down in the future) and passing a junction, continue forward along the main road. Leave the end of the speed restriction zone signs behind and,

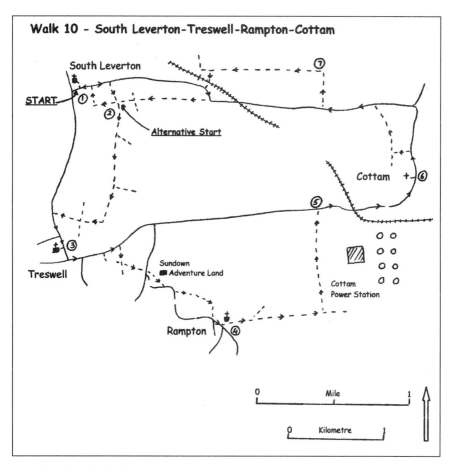

Walk 10 - South Leverton-Treswell-Rampton-Cottam

immediately before a red-brick dormer bungalow with steep roof on your right, go right onto a green lane with hedges to either side. Continue for about 200m and at a two-way finger-post, go left through a (sometimes gated) hedge gap into field corner. Cross diagonally right, aiming for the bottom corner of the field, or if this is not visible, then aim immediately to the right of the garage of a red-brick house, which can be seen in the distance. (We actually cross two fields, usually planted with different crops with a shallow embankment at the join). Pass through a finger-posted hedge gap onto road and go straight over, climbing a finger-posted stile into field corner. Bear diagonally right over the field ahead, aiming for a wide gap in the far hedge and here, bear gently right again, over the Sundown Adventure Land car park, aiming for the left-hand of the two car park entrances to arrive on another road. Go left along the road and follow it through a sharp bend to the right passing the Rampton village sign then go left over finger-posted stile into field corner. Go forward with a hedge to your right and, where the hedge comes to an end, bear gently right over the field aiming for the far field corner; this is well to the left of the distant church tower and at a point where a line of trees joins a hedgeline. Cross the stile in the field corner and bear right, with hedge to the right and paddock left, to climb another stile and go forward again to join an access drive that leads to the road in Rampton. Go left through the village, passing the 'Tudor' gateway to your left, then bear left onto Torksey Street with the church to your left.

Rampton today is overshadowed by the huge cooling towers of Cottam Power Station. In the past it has been the home of noble families, in particular, the de Ramptons who moved here in the 12th century and, in more recent times, the Eyres, whose monuments can be found in the church. In Domesday Book, the area appears as 'Rametone', from the Old English meaning the 'farmstead where rams are kept'. The gateway on the approach to the church occupies the site of one of the entrances to the old manor house, but this is a 19th-century replica. The 'real' version, hidden in the grounds of the adjacent churchyard, is much more impressive, though much worn. Dating from the early Tudor period, it is adorned with panels containing the coats-of-arms of the various owners of the Manor and Hall. These include the de Ramptons themselves, the Malovels, Stanhopes, Babingtons and Eyres, all descendants of the first owner. The old Hall was demolished in 1736 when the family moved to Grove and was replaced by a mock-Tudor building in 1851 which was reoccupied by family members until their final departure at the end of the last century. Now the building has been heavily renovated and converted into flats. All Saints' beautifully proportioned slim west tower is unusual for this part of Nottinghamshire in that it is Early English rather than Perpendicular. The tower is topped with battlements that stand a little proud of the tower itself but the remainder of the building is completely plain. The west window is 15th century, as is the south porch, with its much later sundial but the south doorway is Early English. The south windows are very tall and square and probably date from the 17th or 18th centuries. Inside the church is a fine Norman font bowl on a 15th-century pedestal, though a pillar and some masonry in the north wall might date from Saxon times. The north arcade dates from around 1300, while that to the south is about a hundred years later. There are a number of memorials to the Eyre family, including one to Sir Gervase who died defending Newark for the Royalists in the Civil War, another to Admiral Sir George who died in 1839 having fought in the French wars, Sir William who served in the Crimea and Anthony, his only son, killed in the Ashanti War.

4. Return to Torksey Street and go left, with the church over the wall to your left. Ignore all side paths and continue for just over half a mile, the

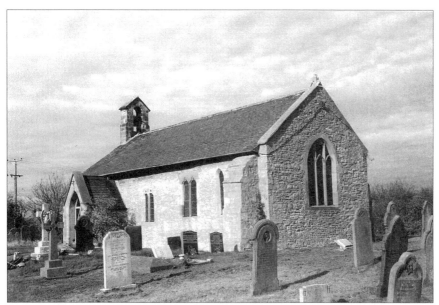

Holy Trinity, Cottam

bulk of Cottam Power Station ahead and to the left. About 200m before a mass of overhead power cables, go left onto a finger-posted footpath with the power station perimeter fence to your right.

Cottam is the middle of the three power stations that are constantly in our view when walking in the east and central sections of North Nottinghamshire. At first sight, they may be dismissed as awful blots on the landscape, but in different strengths of sunlight or shade, or half shrouded by early morning mist, they can adopt a strange man-made beauty. Whatever they are though, they are overpowering, especially from close up as we see Cottam on today's walk. Cottam started generating in 1969 and its eight massive cooling towers, each 114m high, can cool 1,300 million gallons of water every hour.

Continue along what becomes a lovely shaded path between trees and bushes, crossing two footbridges and eventually arriving on a road.

5. Go right along the road with the power station to your right and climb the gentle incline over the railway tracks to enter the long drawn-out village of Cottam. Pass the Moth & Lantern hotel to your left and follow Town Street as it bends sharply left to pass a telephone box and the Wesleyan chapel with the date 1857. 100m on, go left through a double wooden gateway with the parish notice board beside it which leads to a path along the edge of a garden hedge and stable buildings to the church.

Although dominated by the massive power station cooling towers, Cottam is a typical North Nottinghamshire village. It has some fine farmhouses, a lovely little church and an excellent inn. It does not get a mention in Domesday Book but appears as 'Cotum' in a document of 1274. The name is derived from the Old English meaning '(the place at) the cottages or huts'. Holy Trinity has suffered greatly from neglect and attempted restorations of 1869 and 1890. Today it is a single box combining nave and chancel with single bellcote and south porch inside which is a magnificent Norman doorway with chevron decoration. At the south-east end of the building is an old buttress but, going round to the north side there is a real hotchpotch of repairs – more recent buttressing and patched up walls together with partially revealed sealed arcades. There is a sealed door in the west front and a nice west window although the building has a real mixture of window types. Lying in the grass beside the porch is an old font tub and plinth.

6. Return to Town Street and go left along the road, passing out of the village. As the road bends to the right, go left onto a finger-posted track with dog kennels to your left. At a T-junction, go right along another track that leads between fields with the towers of West Burton Power Station in the distance ahead, to arrive on a narrow country lane. Go left along the lane for about 600m, then, more or less opposite the end of the Cottam Power Station buildings way over to your left, leave the road to go right along a green lane which becomes a path between open fields. At the top field corner, pass over a culvert and through a gap between hedges and trees then go immediately left onto a green lane with a hedge to your right and trees left.

7. We keep to this line now for about three-quarters of a mile as our route sometimes retains its green lane status and at others, becomes little more than a headland path, with occasional glimpses of the church towers of Sturton le Steeple and North Leverton in the distance to the front right. At a wide hedge gap to your left, leave the main track and go left on another green lane which leads us to a railway crossing (cross with care) and onto a surfaced lane. Go left then right with the lane and where the lane bends sharply to the left again, go right onto another green lane (Meadow Dike Lane). Where the main lane bends off to the left, go forward on a lesser track to cross the deep Catchwater Drain and continue to the crossing which was our alternative parking area. Go forward over the junction and stay with the track until it joins the end of a surfaced cul-de-sac. Here, go right onto a driveway and continue forward along a narrow pathway between garden hedges/fences then through a very narrow gap onto Town Street in South Leverton. Go left to the Village Hall and our start point.

11. East Retford – Babworth – West Retford

Distance: 10 miles (16km)

Maps: OS Landranger 120: Mansfield & Worksop, Sherwood Forest. OS Explorer 28: Sherwood Forest (to be renumbered 270); 271: Newark-on-Trent; Retford, Southwell & Saxilby; 279: Doncaster; Conisbrough, Maltby & Thorne

Start: St Swithun's church, East Retford (GR 706813). It is difficult to find parking in Retford which is not pay-and-display; perhaps the most convenient for our walk is Church Gate Car Park which is just off Amcott Way and west of the church. Alternatively, the walk might be started at Babworth where there is ample (free) parking beside the church.

Churches: St Swithun, East Retford; All Saints, Babworth; St Michael, West Retford

The Walk

A fine walk which can be undertaken at any time of the year. We start in the historic market town of Retford, take in some lovely canal towpath, a long section of green lane, some cross-field and town walking and visit three magnificent churches. The greatest problem with this walk is the quantity of large-scale mapping required to cover it!

Retford is recorded as 'Redforde' in Domesday Book, coming from the Old English meaning 'red ford'. Today's town is made up of East and West Retford, separated by the River Idle, and what was once the village of Ordsall – now a south-western suburb; fortunately, all retain their own distinctive churches. West Retford is the older part of the town with East Retford being established in about 1105 by King Henry I so that tolls could be collected from those crossing the river at this point. West Retford grew in importance when it was granted a market charter by King Henry III in 1246. Despite a great fire, which destroyed much of the settlement in 1528, East Retford slowly outgrew its western neighbour. Both prospered with the routing of the Great North Road through the town in 1766, the completion of the Chesterfield Canal in 1777 and the arrival of the railway in 1849. These advancements resulted in some fine Georgian and Victorian buildings and now, happily, the Great North Road has again been diverted so leaving this lovely market town in peace. Our walk begins at the church of St Swithun, East Retford. This is a magnificent cruciform building, bristling with battle-

St Swithun, East Retford

ments, gargoyles and crocketed pinnacles. It is said to have been founded by Roger, Archbishop of York in 1258 but, as the result of a tower collapse in 1651 which demolished much of the structure, most of what we see today is the result of a 1658 restoration and a Victorian rebuild. The north transept though is of the original Medieval building and the internal nave arcades are partly 14th century. The northern side of the church was largely rebuilt in 1855 when the north and south porches were added.

The Route

1. Return to Chapel Gate and continue past the Sebastopol Cannon, then bear left into the Market Place.

The Sebastopol Cannon dates from 1855 and is a 2 ton 24 pounder, brought to Retford to celebrate victory in the Crimean War. It arrived in the town in 1858 but arguments raged over where it should be sited and it was another year before it was placed in its current location and given the name 'Earl of Aberdeen' after the Prime Minister of the time. During the Second World War it was to have been melted down but was saved by a local solicitor who bought and hid it until the end of hostilities.

The Market Square was laid down in the late 18ᵗʰ century following the routing of the Great North Road through the town and this resulted in its fine collection of Georgian buildings. It will well repay a visit, perhaps guided by the pamphlet available from the Tourist Information office in Grove Street but, for the moment, note especially the fine war memorial in the centre with distances marked to battle sites of the First World War and, on the south side, the chateau-look-alike Town Hall. This was built in 1868 to replace a Georgian structure. In front of the Town Hall is a stone known as the Broad Stone, probably the base of an old parish boundary cross which was moved here in the early 1800s. Tradition has it that in the plague years, coins for trading were placed in vinegar in the hollow of the stone to prevent disease from spreading to those whose goods were bought with them.

Keep the main square to your right and, passing over Grove Street, continue down Carolgate. Pass Exchange Street and Coronation Street to your right then take the next right (West Street). Pass Carr Road and, at the major junction with The White Lion inn to your left, go forward over the road with great care and continue down the West Street extension. Our route takes us over the River Idle bridge and becomes a pleasant path through King's Park with views of the crocketed spire of St Michael's over to the right. Continue forward to mount the sloping walk-way ahead and, where this bends sharply to the right, drop down steps to the canal bank.

2. Go forward along the towpath passing beneath an unnumbered bridge then West Retford Lock and continuing with the canal to your left. We stay with the canal now for a little over 3½ miles (6 km) as it passes beneath bridges 55, 54B, 54A and 54 where there are distant views of Sutton church tower far to the right. We pass Forest Bottom Lock, Forest Mid Bottom Lock and Forest Middle Top Lock, where there are long-term moorings for barges. Then, go forward along a short section of surfaced lane before the towpath reverts to a pleasant footpath and passes beneath Bridge No 53. Continue past Forest Top Lock to the next bridge (No 52).

3. Walk beneath the bridge then go quickly right, up the embankment, then right again, over the bridge and the canal and follow a fine green lane (Green Mile Lane). Pass a group of cottages at the junction with the Old London Road and go straight over, picking up the gently undulating continuation of the lane. Half a mile beyond the crossing we pass an area of woodland to our left then the lane dips and mounts gently. Ignore the track, which bends off to the left, and continue with woodland to either side. *Just before the far end of the woodland to your left*, go left, onto a finger-posted footpath signed 'Babworth Church – ¾ mile'. The path

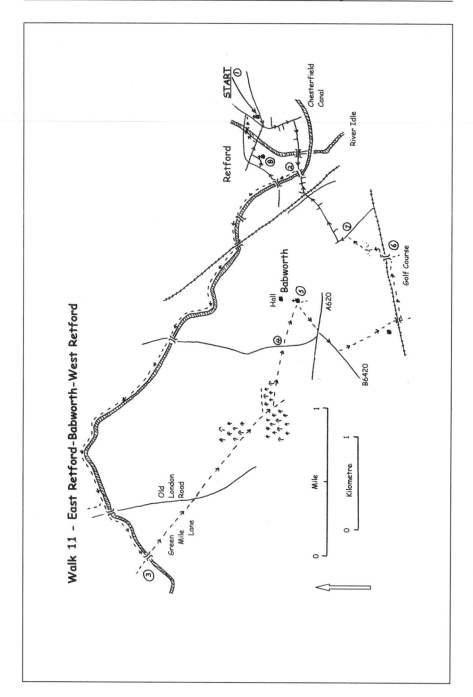

Walk 11 - East Retford-Babworth-West Retford

continues with woodland to the left and thick hedge right. At a track-crossing, go forward over a stile then continue the line of walk over grassland to another stile where we bear gently left to pass to the left of a wooded enclosure and arrive at another stile onto a country road.

4. Cross the road with care, passing through a wide hedge gap and following the direction of the finger-post which indicates 'Babworth Church – ¼ mile'. This takes us gently upwards over the field with a copse over to the right. Cross the stile at the top of the field (where we get a glimpse of Babworth Hall ahead) and follow the path over scrub with a fence to the right to enter woodland. The path drops down amongst the trees to the delightfully secluded church of All Saints.

Babworth was 'Baburde' in Domesday Book and comes from the Old English meaning 'the enclosure of a man called Babba'. Today it is a tiny settlement, its fame lying in its link with the Pilgrim Fathers who sailed in the Mayflower to the New World in 1620. Richard Clyfton was Rector of the church here from 1586 until 1604, but he became increasingly non-conformist in his views and in 1605 was in trouble with his bishops, eventually being deprived of the living. William Brewster, a leader of the 'Separatists', offered him hospitality at his home, Scrooby Manor. Clyfton preached informally at Babworth and Bawtry before sailing with the pilgrims to Holland. He died in Amsterdam in 1616, four years before Brewster and his followers sailed to Plymouth, New England to found their colony. Babworth Hall, originally the home of the Elwes family (of Saundby), was acquired by William Simpson at the end of the 17th century and remained in the family possession until the end of the 19th. John Bridgeman Simpson, younger son of the 1st Lord Bradford succeeded his uncle in 1768 and it was he who employed Humphrey Repton to transform the house and its surroundings between 1795 and 1820; this is, basically, the building we glimpse today. All Saints is beautifully sited amongst trees and is set well back from the nearest road. It is a plain church and a fairly typical North Nottinghamshire Perpendicular building. It has a relatively short battlemented tower with corner crocketed pinnacles with additional battlements and pinnacles adorning the combined nave and chancel, substantial north aisle and the large south porch. Restorations of 1859 and 1877 fortunately did little damage to the original building. In the porch a plaque recalls a visit in 1955 by the General Society of Mayflower descendants of America. The churchyard contains a number of thought-provoking gravestones including one to Millicent, the wife of Jerimiah Rogers who died in 1791, aged 25 and her infant son 'whose breath did cause the tender mother's death'. This was a sadly afflicted family since nearby lies the body of Sarah, a daughter of the couple who died in 1788 aged one month, and John, their son, who passed away in 1790 aged 2 months.

5. Leave the church by the path that runs south-westwards from the porch to drop down steps and through a gateway onto a lane. Go forward along the lane with our approach route to the right and, to our left, a car parking area then the grounds of Haygarth House, and continue to the busy A620. Cross the road with care, and continue along the pavement of the B6420 opposite, signed to Apley Head and Clumber. Follow the road for 300m then, at the top of the gentle incline, cross to go left beside a power post along a finger-posted lane signed to Great Morton Farm. Follow the lane as it meanders past the farm buildings then continues as a stony track to pass beneath a railway bridge. Immediately after the bridge, go left along a headland track with the railway embankment up to your left to arrive at the edge of the golf course. Keep well over to the left, close against the railway embankment/cutting, as the path climbs gently, keeping a wary eye for flying golf balls!

6. At the top of the slope (there is a false crest), pass through a hedge gap then go left over a footbridge crossing the railway then right with the railway now in a cutting down to your right and woodland left. At the wood end, beside a power post, go left along a path with the trees over to your left and playing fields right to arrive on a tree-lined lane. Cross the lane into the corner of a sports field and bear diagonally right over the field, aiming for the far corner with the sports pavilion over to the right. At the far field corner, bear right into a little alleyway between house gardens and onto Ordsall Road.

7. Go left for about 100m then right into Ordsall Park Road and continue all the way to the junction with West Carr Road. Cross the road with care and continue over the railway footbridge opposite. At the far side, bear right then left onto a lane (Pelham Road) barred to traffic by concrete posts. Go over the cross-roads and continue down Pelham Road, passing a school to your left and, where the road swings right as Cobwell Road, go straight on to the Chesterfield Canal. Cross the canal then go left, dropping down to the towpath and rejoining our outward route (paragraph 2 above). Pass beneath the unnumbered bridge and beside West Retford Lock then mount the steps at the next bridge (No 55) to join Hospital Road. Go right along the road (note the hospital building over to the left which dates from between 1832 and 1872) then go right again into Rectory Road which swings to the left and brings us to West Retford's magnificent church.

St Michael is a fine Medieval building with a slim west tower with battlements and corner crocketed pinnacles topped by a magnificent and most unusual 14th-century crocketed spire supported by mini flying buttresses. The north aisle was added during a restoration of 1863 but was built in the Decorated style while that to the south, although again heavily restored, is still genuinely Perpendicular and sports a very large porch. The chancel is also part of the 1863 restoration and retains little of its original form. This is very much an Anglo-Catholic church with massive interior adornment. In the gardens there is a fine memorial to Charles Gray, who was variously Canon at Southwell, East Retford, Blyth, and West Retford during the latter part of the 19th century and for the first nineteen years of the 20th. Perhaps the only spoiling feature of this magnificent building is the tasteless add-on church hall built onto the south-east end.

8. Leave the church and go right to the junction with Bridgegate, the Galway Arms inn opposite. Go right along the road, passing the Newcastle Arms to your right then immediately before crossing the River Idle road bridge, go left, down a surfaced footpath, passing Riverside House to your right. Continue with the River Idle to your right then, immediately before the road bridge, go right, over the wooden footbridge and back into Church Gate Car Park. To return to the start point, walk diagonally left across the car park and just before the Amcott Road entrance, bear right into Church Gate and so to the church of St Swithun.

12. Eaton – Ordsall

Distance: 5 miles (8km)

Maps: OS Landranger 120: Mansfield & Worksop, Sherwood Forest. OS Explorer 271: Newark-on-Trent; Retford, Southwell & Saxilby

Start: Limited parking immediately to the south of the railway crossing at Eaton Lane where the path runs eastwards to Eaton Wood (GR 723779).

Churches: All Saints, Eaton; All Hallows, Ordsall

The Walk

A short stroll today and despite a lengthy section of road walking, a pleasant one nevertheless. Country lanes take us to Eaton and its unusual little church then field paths and the banks of the River Idle lead us into Ordsall. More roads, farm track and a cross-field path eventually bring us to the edge of Eaton Wood where we drop gently back to our start point.

The Route

1. *Walk away from the railway line* and back onto the road to continue forward along this little used highway for about half a mile and arrive at the busy A638. Go left here for a few metres then, crossing with the greatest of care, go right, signed to Eaton, passing the college buildings on the corner to your right and entering the tiny village. Continue with the meandering lane to the church.

   Eaton appears as 'Etune' in Domesday Book and comes from the Old English meaning 'the farmstead by the river' in this case, the River Idle which we shall be crossing a couple of times during our walk. There is little in Eaton today apart from some attractive residences, the church and the Hall. This latter once belonged to the estate of the Dukes of Newcastle but was sold in 1919. During the Second World War, it was used as a maternity hospital for the wives of servicemen and, later, as a teacher training college. Today it serves as a conference centre, but is much run down. Perched on top of its grassy mound, All Saints is a strange little building of high porch, chancel and nave with a centrally-placed spirelet perched on the nave roof. It is a very plain building, which lacks aisles but has a fine east window that dates from 1874. In fact, the church is an 1860 rebuild of a much older building which once stood here.

2. Return to the road and go left, crossing the hump-backed bridge over the River Idle and continue over a tiny dike bridge. Turn right here onto a

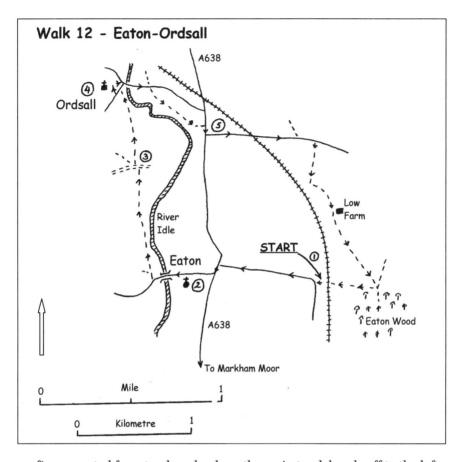

Walk 12 - Eaton-Ordsall

A638

④ Ordsall

⑤

③

River Idle

Low Farm

START ①

Eaton

②

A638

To Markham Moor

Eaton Wood

| Mile | |
| 0 | 1 |

| Kilometre | |
| 0 | 1 |

finger-posted farm track and, where the main track bends off to the left, go straight on, as waymarked, along a headland path with a ditch down to your right. Follow the ditch as it eventually swings to the left to cross a footbridge at the field corner then go right, along the headland, with a hedge and ditch to your right. Stay on this path now to a green lane crossing.

3. [The definitive path goes left here for about 10m then right, through a hedge gap then forward over a section of field to join the end of a hedgeline which comes in from the front. The commonly walked path however goes straight over the green lane and follows the ditch edge as it bends left to join the definitive line at the hedge]. Continue with the hedge/treeline to your right, soon bearing left and away from the dike on a well-walked path, which leads to the edge of a house garden. Go forward over gardens (the pathline is beautifully waymarked) with houses up to your left to eventually pass through a wicket gate and onto the banks of the River Idle. Stay with the river bank, passing through a double field gate and then, a couple of hundred metres before the road bridge ahead, bear left with garages right, over a driveway and onto a road. Go left for 100m and, with The Plough inn to the left, go right up Church Lane and so to the lovely building of All Hallows.

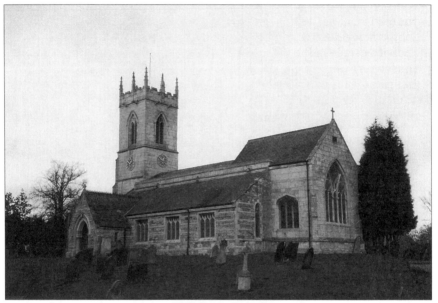

All Hallows, Ordsall

Today, Ordsall is little more than a suburb of Retford but originally it was a village in its own right. In Domesday Book, it is given as 'Ordeshale', probably meaning 'the land in a hollow or in a river bend belonging to Ord'. All Hallows is a fine Perpendicular-style building with its slim battlemented tower topped with corner and intervening crocketed pinnacles, nave, very tall chancel and aisles to north and south. Inside, the nave arcades can be dated to the 13th century. There is a fine 15th-century screen and a plain octagonal font which was presented to the church in 1877. (The older, original font is at the east end of the south aisle). The south aisle was apparently widened and the tower partially rebuilt in 1876 and there was further restoration four years later, but internally, this is a building bursting with interesting features and, especially, memorials. In the north aisle is a fine monument believed to be to Samuel Bevercotes who died in 1603 and a magnificent window to John Shadrach Piercy who wrote the *History of Retford* with an account of Ordsall village in 1828 and who died in 1868. In the south aisle, there are more monuments and floor stones from the 17th and 18th centuries, including a link to Ossington through the Brownelow family. On a wall, there is a list of Rectors going back to William de Bliburg (1277).

4. Leave the church by the surfaced pathway which drops down steps through the east end of the churchyard to pass through the lych gate and onto a road (All Hallows Street). Go right then take the first left (Goosemoor Lane), crossing the River Idle road bridge. Continue along the road for about 300m then go right over a stile and onto a finger-posted footpath, walking diagonally left over wasteland and aiming for the blue roof of a garage in the distance. Soon, we pick up the perimeter fence of the football pitch to our left and continue over more wasteland to a kissing gate which takes us between garden fences/hedges and along the front of houses onto the busy London Road (A638).

5. Go right, along the road for 100m, then, crossing with the greatest of care, go left, signed to Grove, Headon and Rampton. Pass over the Grove Road railway crossing and 500m further on (take care along this section – there are minimal verges), go right onto a finger-posted farm track. The track meanders towards Low Farm but, immediately before the farm complex, drop down the embankment to your right and continue forward with a hedge up to the left and farm buildings beyond. Pass beside double power posts with junction box and, at the external hedge corner, go diagonally left, climbing the gentle incline of the field and aiming for the thickest part of the woodland on the horizon. As we crest the slope, look over to the top *left-hand* corner of the field where a hedgeline will be seen coming in from the left to join the wood. This join should be our aiming point if the path is not well-defined. At the wood edge, pass through the narrow gap to the right and, ignoring the stile to the front which leads into the trees (we shall pass this way in Walk 13) go immediately right onto a grassy track with woodland to your left and screen of bushes/trees to the right. This is a lovely path which, leaving the edge of Eaton Wood behind, continues between bushes then drops gently with fine views of Retford and Ordsall churches over to the front right. Soon we arrive at the railway line – cross with the greatest of care – and so back at our start point.

13. Eaton/Gamston Wood – Askham – Upton – Headon – Grove

Distance: 8 miles (13km)

Maps: OS Landranger 120: Mansfield & Worksop, Sherwood Forest. OS Explorer 271: Newark-on-Trent; Retford, Southwell & Saxilby

Start: Verge parking along the Eaton-Upton road adjacent to Eaton/Gamston Wood. Note that if you use one of the woodland access points, care should be taken not to block the way for forestry vehicles. If in doubt, park on the verge at the northern end of Causeway Lane where it meets the Upton-Eaton road (GR 726772).

Churches: St Nicholas, Askham; St Peter, Headon; St Helen, Grove

The Walk

A stroll over and around fields, along quiet country lanes and through some old woodland, taking in three fine churches. This is one of those walks where the most obvious cross-field paths depicted on maps are not always practicable and therefore there is a little more road walking than might seem necessary.

We start amongst a lovely area of mixed broadleaf and conifer woodland which is owned by the Nottinghamshire Wildlife Trust and which is open to the public. Eaton Wood was actually recorded in Domesday Book as pasture woodland and there are still examples of ridge and furrow to be seen here.

The Route

1. Walk eastwards along the road in the direction of Upton with Gamston Wood to your right and Eaton Wood to the left. Leaving Eaton Wood behind, continue with trees to the right and where these come to an end beside a telegraph post, go right onto a finger-posted lane with a house hiding behind trees to your left. [Note: at the time of writing, the direct route to Askham church was not suitable for comfortable walking therefore please follow the directions given below]. Follow the track as it drops gently then, where an access track goes off to the left beside a telegraph post, go left, as waymarked, along a narrow footpath which runs to the right of and parallel to the track, separated from it by bushes. Here we begin to get distant views to the front right of Askham church tower. Pass the farm buildings over to your left and continue along a headland path

Walk 13 - Eaton/Gamston Wood-Askham-Upton-Headon-Grove

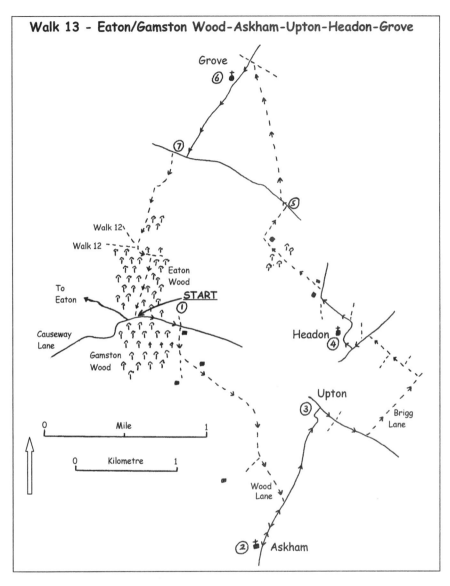

with hedgeline to the left. At the field corner, go left over a little plank bridge and then immediately right, still with the headland but with a hedge now to your right. [Note: a waymarker a short distance to the front as you cross the 'bridge' takes you over the field parallel to the headland route described below. The described route is much easier to follow and will result in less damage to crops]. Stay with the headland as it swings to the right and left, losing the hedge for a short distance but soon recovering it to arrive eventually at the end of a green lane (Wood Lane). Go forward, ignoring all side tracks, eventually to join the Upton road.

The main walk continues to the left along the road here but a short detour to the attractive church at Askham is well worth the effort. Unfortunately, the footpath access to the village is not always easy, therefore a visit will involve a quarter-mile walk up the road to the right and a return by the same route. The village is given as 'Ascam' in Domesday Book, coming from the Old English meaning 'the homestead/enclosure where ash trees grow'. Its fine church, dedicated to St Nicholas, is approached by a lychgate, erected to commemorate the Silver Jubilee of King George V in 1935 and has the inscription 'Eventide brings all home'. The Perpendicular tower is battlemented with eight crocketed pinnacles and there is an aisleless nave which has some Norman masonry in the south wall and a plain 13th-century chancel from which time can also be dated the fine east window. The south porch was added during a restoration of 1906.

2. If you have visited Askham church, return back down the hill and, passing the junction with Wood Lane, continue forward along the road which rises gently then flattens to give views ahead of Headon church tower with, at various angles to the right, the cooling towers of two of the Trent Valley power stations and, on a clear day, far over to the right, the towers of Lincoln Cathedral. (This road has very limited verges and although few vehicles are likely to be encountered, take the greatest of care when walking it). The road eventually drops through an S-bend into the centre of Upton.

3. Go right at the junction, signed to East Drayton and Dunham, noting the old AA village sign affixed to the wall of the red brick barn to your right. It gives, amongst other information, the distance to London as 142 miles! Continue out of the hamlet, ignoring finger-posted footpaths to left and right, passing the end of speed restriction signs then a lone house to your left. Some 50m beyond the house, leave the road to go left onto a stony track — hedge to the left and embankment with railings up to your right, where a sign announces that there is a weak bridge a quarter of a mile ahead! Almost immediately, we join a green lane (Brigg Lane) which takes us on over the hardly noticeable 'weak bridge' then slowly climbs between hedges. Half a mile on, the lane does a sharp turn to the left and we go with it to emerge, eventually, beside farm buildings and out onto a road at the edge of Headon. Go left, down the road, and near the bottom of the slope go right signed to Grove and Retford, climbing gently to the steps and gateway that lead into the churchyard.

St Peter, Headon

In Domesday Book, Headon is given as 'Hedune' which comes from the Old English meaning 'high hill' – a just description. The village was the home of the Wasteneys family from the 14th century until the last male heir died in 1742 but the Hall where the family lived is no more. Today Headon is a tiny, tidy village, the church of St Peter being a truly impressive building, with a stubby tower dating from the Early English period although the battlements are probably part of a 19th-century restoration. The north and south arcades are of the same age but the remainder of this unadorned building is Perpendicular, with lovely windows in the aisles and clerestory. Fascinating, though, are the huge sealed arches set in the north and south faces of the tower which might indicate much larger aisles at one time.

4. Return to the road and go left. Pass the village hall (private parking) and walk out of the village down a road with minimal verges where care must be taken when the infrequent vehicle is heard. Ignoring all finger-posted routes to left and right, follow the road as it swings to the right at the bottom of the slope and runs along the front of farm buildings over to your left. Immediately before overhead power cables, go left, through a finger-posted wicket gate and into a house garden. Keep well over to the left with a hedge to your left to cross the bottom of the garden and emerge through a gap into a field. Go forward, aiming for a line of trees in the middle of the field. Continue beside the tree line then, at their end, stay on your line, over the field, to enter woodland. Pass through a narrow strip of trees to emerge onto a wide green way with woodland to either side. Go forward, to pass a farm building on the right (with dogs who guard their property noisily) and onto a farm track. Go right and continue all the way to a relatively busy road.

5. Go left along the road for a little under 100m (take great care – there are no verges) then, immediately beyond the first hedgeline that comes in to the road from the right, go right, over a finger-posted stile and into a field corner. Walk diagonally left over this large field, aiming initially towards the right-hand tree-top, which pokes over the skyline (a power post is virtually on the same line). The line of the path soon changes slightly so that we are now aiming for the mid-way point between the power post and a huge communications mast in the far distance. Pass beneath power lines and continue your line, the roof tops of Grove soon appearing to the front and, a little to their left, the spire of Grove church. At the field edge, cross a stile and continue the line over the next field, aiming for the bottom corner where there is a wide (gated) hedge gap. Cross the stile beside the gap and continue over the next field aiming towards field gates at the far side. Cross the stile here and again, continue the original line, to arrive at a stile in the field corner with red-brick garage building to your left. Cross onto a lane and go left to Main Street in the village of Grove. Go over the road to the pavement at the far side and go left, gently down slope, passing steps up to the war memorial. Stay with the pavement which keeps parallel to, but above the level of, the road and so to the lych-gate entrance to the church.

Grove is a tiny village lacking shops and inns and even its fine 16ᵗʰ/17ᵗʰ-century Hall, originally the home of the Hercys but later of the Neville, Levinz, Eyre and Harcourt-Vernon families, was demolished in 1951. In Domesday Book, it appears as 'Grava', taking its name from the Old English meaning '(the place at) the copse or grove'. The church of St Helen was built in the Decorated style in 1882 and is rather plain, with only the tower adorned by battlements, gargoyles and corner, crocketed, pinnacles but is topped by a fine recessed spire. The tower clock has the inscription 'Watch and pray' and mounted above the south porch is an effigy of St Helen. Internally, the church is again fairly plain, lacking arcades and aisles but there is a fine octagonal font. It is at the west end that history is revealed for here, removed from the original building which stood close by, there are some fine gravestones set in the floor. A wall tablet explains that "Below is the tomb of Sir Hugh Hercy of Grove, Notts, who died in December 1455 and his wife Elizabeth, daughter of Sir Simon Leke of Cottam, Notts, who died in 1450. It was moved from the chancel of the old church and placed here in 1882…". Take a look in the little notebook used for visitors' signatures – it goes back to August 1939!

6. Return to Main Street and go right, dropping down the road and out of the village (with care since the pavement soon comes to an end and there are minimal verges). Continue for about half a mile to a T-junction with a major road.

7. Go right, signed to Retford, for about 150m, then left, through a metal gateway and onto a farm track with a hedge to your right. Pass a patch of woodland to your left and continue along what becomes a headland path with hedge to your right and Eaton Wood ahead. Just before the wood edge, go right through a wide hedge gap then immediately left through a much narrower space in the hedge. Cross a track (we passed this way in Walk 12) and then a stile beside fieldgate into the trees to pick up a path that goes straight ahead. At a T-junction of paths, go left, with the waymarker, onto a major track and, about 150m along, beside a muddy puddle in the trees to your right, ignore the waymarker, which directs ahead and go right on a major (permissive) pathway/ride which gradually rises through the trees. Ignore all side tracks and go straight on to join a major farm track which comes in from the right. Keep the same direction forward until you pass through a gap beside a gate and out onto the road where our walk began.

14. Laneham – Stokeham – East Drayton – Church Laneham

Distance: 8¾ miles (14km)

Maps: OS Landranger 120: Mansfield & Worksop, Sherwood Forest, 121: Lincoln & Newark on Trent. OS Explorer 271: Newark-on-Trent; Retford, Southwell & Saxilby

Start: Ample parking on the grass verges of the Trent bank north of Church Laneham. If possible, park close to the entrance to Manor House Caravan Park (GR 815771). Note that there are parking restrictions along the road here between 16th March and 1st November, but provided you "park prettily", and off the road, there should be no problem.

Churches: St Peter, Stokeham; St Peter, East Drayton; St Peter, Church Laneham

---

The Walk

Three fine churches, all dedicated to St Peter, are visited in today's walk. Starting from the banks of the River Trent, green lanes and tracks take us to Stokeham with its little bellcoted church. Cross-field paths and a short section of country lane lead us on to the wonderful Perpendicular building at East Drayton before more fieldpaths, green lanes and country roads bring us back to the magnificent Norman church at Church Laneham, close to our start point.

Our walk begins in the tiny village of Church Laneham, which is sepa-rated from its larger neighbour by the Laneham Beck. Church Laneham has the village church, a fine building with significant Norman remnants, which we shall visit at the end of our journey. The area was spelt 'Lanum' in Domesday Book and comes from the Old English meaning '(the place at) the lanes'. Today's village is just that – a lovely quiet spot nestling up against the Trent and criss-crossed by green lanes, minor country roads, footpaths and bridleways.

The Route

1. Walk into the entrance to Manor House Caravan Park and as directed by the finger post, bear left, with hedge (road over) to your left and the house itself up to the right. Aim for the point at which the embankment to your right meets the far hedgeline where a kissing gate takes us through onto a

bridleway with a dike barrier ahead. Go right here, with a hedge to your right and beck down to the left. Where the dike swings off to the left, go forward to mount the low embankment and arrive on a major track. Go left along the track and continue to a road (Laneham Main Street).

2. Go right into the village of Laneham, passing the Village Hall (unsuitable for parking) and the Methodist chapel (built in 1834). A few metres beyond the telephone box over the road to the left, (and before arriving opposite The Butcher's Arms) go right onto Broading Lane with the war memorial on the corner. Stay with the main lane as it leaves the village behind and deteriorates to a dirt and asphalt surface, passing Holly Folly Farm to your right and eventually reaching a country lane with Broading Farm (kennels and cattery) on the corner to the right. As we walk along here, the skyline to the front right is dominated by the cooling towers of Cottam Power Station and Rampton church tower can be glimpsed in the distance ahead.

3. Go left along the lane to the junction with Rampton Road then straight over onto a green lane (Salins Lane). We stay with this lovely track for about a mile (it changes its name to Wranglands Lane about half way along its length) with, soon, views of Rampton Hospital over to the front right and, when the leaves are off the trees, the bellcote of Stokeham church glimpsed to the front left, eventually arriving at the relatively busy Rampton-Laneham road.

4. Go left along the road (cross with care to a pavement on the far side) and after about 200m, go right, signed to Stokeham and Retford. Ignore the road left signed to East Drayton and continue through the village to the church.

Stokeham appears in Domesday Book as 'Estoches' but by 1242 it's as 'Stokum', the name coming from the Old English meaning '(the place at) the outlying farmstead'. The church of St Peter is an attractive little building despite attempts to ravish it through 'restorations', the worst of these being in 1928. Today, there is just a nave and chancel which probably date from the 13th century, the west end being topped by a double bellcote with just one bell. A south aisle was pulled down in the 17th or 18th century but the three original arcades can clearly be seen, one filled with an ashlared porch (beside which lies an old stone coffin), the other two filled with dreadful squared windows. In the north wall of the nave is a sealed doorway and at the west end, a window sits in what might have been a tower archway. Apart from the south windows already mentioned, the walls are pierced with a real mixture of apertures, the east window dating from the 15th century.

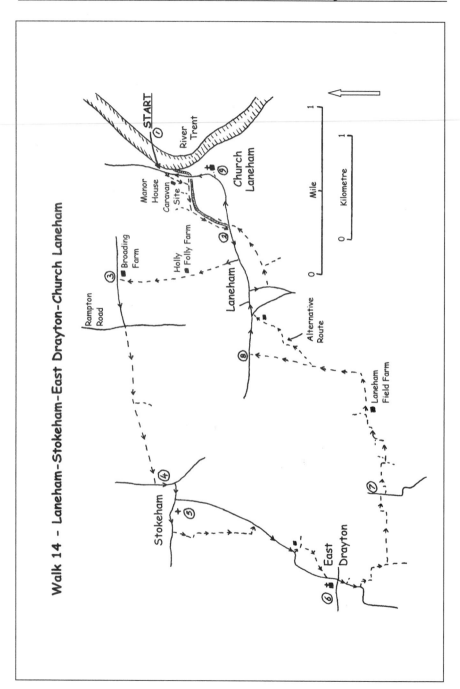

Walk 14 – Laneham-Stokeham-East Drayton-Church Laneham

5. Return to the road and go left, passing out of the village and the end of speed restriction signs. Just before the last red-brick house to your right, go left onto a finger-posted track with, initially, hedge to your left and the tower of East Drayton church in the distance ahead. Continue forward along what soon becomes a headland path with a hedge to your right. Follow this headland as it bends left and right around a copse, then continue the original line with a shallow ditch and embankment to your right. Cross the plank bridge at the field corner and bear very slightly left, aiming for the start of a hedgeline in the distance where we continue the line of walk with the hedge to the right. At the field corner, go left onto a track with a hedge to the right to join a minor road. Go right (take care, there are minimal verges) and, where the road makes a sharp bend to the right, go left onto a finger-posted lane. 60m on, go right, over a stile and into the corner of a meadow. Continue with the hedge to your right and at the field corner, cross the stile and bridge to the right and pass into another field edge. Bear right along the headland with a hedge to your right to another stile. Cross into a paddock and bear left, aiming for the far field corner where the hedge/fence join a red brick barn. Here, cross a stile onto road and go left into the village of East Drayton, with the church to your right, and over the road to the left, the Blue Bell Inn.

East Drayton is a most attractive village grouped around its church and nearby inn. Its most famous son was the 17th-century architect Nicholas Hawksmoor who worked with both Christopher Wren and Vanbrugh on projects, which included the Royal Naval College at Greenwich. The village name is spelt as both 'Draitone' and 'Draitun' in Domesday Book but by 1276 we have 'Est Draiton' (the name 'West Draytone' appeared in 1269). Drayton is a fairly common place name, which can mean 'the farmstead near the slope used for dragging down loads' or 'the farmstead where drays or sledges are used'. The church of St Peter is a fine Nottinghamshire Perpendicular-style building with sturdy tower, topped with battlements and eight pinnacles (although at the time of writing, one has been removed). The clerestory and chancel are similarly embattled, as are the north and south aisles and there is an impressively large 16th-century south porch decorated with crocketed pinnacles. Although most of the exterior is of the 14th and 15th centuries, there are 13th-century nave arcades inside the building. This is a plain, bright and light building which possesses a fine 15th-century rood screen with, to the side, an eagle lectern which sits on what is thought to be the tomb of the last of the De Burgh family who owned large tracts of local land at the time of Henry VIII. Propped up against a wall is an interesting lead sheet with an etching of the church dated 1792, which was taken from the nave roof during restoration work in 1982. There is much to see here, but note especially the list of vicars going back to James le Garzun in 1281.

6. Leave the churchyard by the south-east gate and go right to the junction of Low Street, Church Lane and Top Street (The Blue Bell Inn is to the left). Cross straight over the junction and continue up Top Street with the Village Hall (private parking) to your right. Ignore the finger-posted footpath which leads into a driveway left and just before the road swings sharply to the right as Darlton Road, go left beside a wooden field gate onto a grassy lane between house gardens. At the end of the garden hedge to the right, go right along a pathway with beautiful house garden to your right. With barns to the right and lone tree left, go left onto a headland path with a hedge to your left. Continue to the field corner and go right here, keeping the hedge to your left and with views of the little pyramid top of Darlton church in the far distance ahead. After about 150m, at a wide hedge gap, leave the main path and go left, dropping down over a small plank bridge. On the far side is an old gravestone bearing the date 1741. It lies amongst the grass and was presumably removed from the churchyard at some time to be used as a bridge here! Over the bridge, continue forward with the headland, keeping the hedge to your right and at the field corner, cross the plank bridge into the field beyond and continue the line with ditch down to the right. At the next field corner, go right over a plank bridge then left, to continue the original line but with ditch now down to the left. Soon we pick up a hedge to our left and follow the headland as it swings left and right to pass pig sheds over to the left. At the field corner, go right for a few metres then left, through a hedge gap and out onto a country lane.

7. Go right along the lane for a few metres then left onto a finger-posted headland path with a hedge to your right. Just before the external hedge corner, go left on a pathway between fields for 20m and, where a ditch comes in from the right, go right, along the ditch edge with the ditch to your left. At the field corner, go right, with stunted hedge to the left for about 50m. At a wide gap in the hedge, go left onto a wide bridleway with deep ditch down to your right. Continue to the field corner, (ignore the waymarked path left) where we go left. Our path stays with the hedge to the right now as, 150m on, we swing to the right. At the next field corner, go left with trees to your right and, crossing a farmyard access, go right with the hedge to your right, to arrive on a surfaced farm track with (Laneham Field) farm to the right. Go left along the track then right, with the finger-post, skirting farm buildings to your right. Follow the diversion round to the right and arrive on another farm track. [*] Go left along the track (Hoo Lane) and follow it (ignoring all side paths) as it swings left and continues for about three-quarters of a mile to the Stokeham-Laneham road.

[*] A preferred route which avoids a short section of road walking is described below. However, at the time of writing (late January 2001), the County Council had yet to insert a footbridge over a wide dike which bisects the path. Go left along the track (Hoo Lane) and follow it for just over half a mile where a finger-post directs off to the right. Follow the direction of the finger-post which guides diagonally over the field aiming for the large red brick house in the distance. Pass through the hedge gap at the field edge and continue over the next field, now taking the left-hand cooling tower of Cottam Power Station as the aiming point. Cross the dike here by the footbridge and go right, with the dike to your right. Pass through the gap in the hedge that comes in from the left and bear diagonally left over the field beyond, aiming now to the left of the red brick house. At the far field edge, go left with, initially a deep and wide dike to your right then, as the path meanders, a hedge to the right. Leaving the perimeter of the farm behind, continue forward over a section of field to cross a stile onto road. Go left then right into the village of Laneham and rejoin the main route at point [**].

8. Turn right and keep to the wide grass verge of this relatively busy road. Where the main road bears to the right, go left into the village of Laneham. [**] Pass the Rampton road to your left and continue along Main Street for a short distance to go right down Dunham Road, passing the Post Office and shop to your left. Continue to the end of the village and immediately after crossing the road bridge over a dike, go left, crossing a finger-posted stile and follow an embankment path with ditch down to your left. Stay with this path as it keeps close to the beck, crossing several stiles and ignoring tempting side paths that form part of the Trent Valley Way, until arriving at a minor road. Go right along the road to enter the village of Church Laneham and soon, the church.

St Peter's is a wonderful building and a bit of a rarity for Nottinghamshire in that it is very much a Norman structure. Its consists of crenellated tower, nave, the south wall of which is supported by a massive buttress, north aisle and chancel. The tower itself is Norman with Perpendicular 'improvements' and there are fine examples of herringbone work in the chancel, in the south porch and in the nave wall. The south doorway is also Norman, while the porch is a 14th-century timber rarity which was delicately rebuilt in 1932, as indicated by the memorial to one of its builders who died shortly after its completion and who was the first to be carried through it on 2nd July of that year. Inside the building is a very low tower arch and fine Norman chancel arch; the tub font is also of the Norman period. The north aisle arcade is Early English, but the north aisle and chancel windows date from the 14th century. There is a lovely monument dated 1636 to Ellis Markham, a local Justice of the Peace and to his son Gervase, a Captain of Horse, who served

St Peter, Church Laneham

Queen Elizabeth I in the wars in Ireland and the Low Countries. The Markham family are more closely associated with the village of East Markham (see Walk 16) but they once had a mansion here which has unfortunately completely disappeared.

9. Leave the church and go right, down the lane, with the church tower up to the right. Continue with the Ferry Boat Inn to your left and, staying with the road, arrive back at our start point.

15. Elkesley – Bothamsall – Crookford

Distance: 5½ miles (9km)

Maps: OS Landranger 120: Mansfield & Worksop, Sherwood Forest. OS Explorer 28: Sherwood Forest (to be renumbered 270)

Start: Elkesley Village Hall (GR 687754). Ample parking in the village hall car park (entrance opposite the Pottery and signed to Sports Field and Village Hall from High Street) but if more than a couple of cars are to use this facility, please check with the keyholder.

Churches: St Giles, Elkesley; Our Lady and St Peter, Bothamsall

The Walk

A lovely little walk on good tracks and lanes over and around arable fields, through patches of woodland, with two crossings of the River Poulter. This is one of the few walks in the book where we repeat a visit to the same church – in this case, that at Bothamsall, which we meet again in Walk 24. Since the countryside around here is so fine and in any case, the short section is walked in the opposite direction, we shall hardly be aware of the repeat.

We begin at Elkesley, a small village hidden from the hectic A1, 100m to the north. A little under half a mile to the east, but now invisible under the A1, is Twyford Bridge, where the rivers Maun and Meden converge with the Poulter to form the River Idle which eventually meanders north and east to the River Trent. Elkesley appears as 'Elchesleie' in Domesday Book, which means 'the woodland clearing of a man called Ealac', an Old English personal name. We shall soon be walking through part of Ealac's woodland!

The Route

1. Return to High Street and go right along the road for 100m to the church.

St Giles' is approached through a little wooden lych gate that leads to the tower, which once served as a porch. Immediately to the front is a door set into an arch which is obviously much too large for it and this arch is part of the original 15th-century nave arcade. Immediately to the left is another (sealed) archway, left high and dry when the nave was shortened. In the south side of the tower is another 15th-century doorway with a much later door. The tower itself is buttressed, has a fine clock and is topped with battlements and stumpy corner pinnacles – recent additions. The north aisle too is crenellated but there is no such decoration on the clerestory and chancel. The east window dates from the 14th century, but most of the remainder are of about 100 years later. A major rebuild in 1845 accounts for the inconsistencies.

2. Continue along High Street and, opposite the Robin Hood inn, go right
    down Low Street, bearing right into Brough Lane at the junction with
    Park Lane. After about 600m, where the lane makes a significant bend to
    the right and just beyond a metal field gate, go left (the Robin Hood Way)
    onto a headland path with post and wire fence to your left. The path
    drops to a footbridge over the River Poulter and into Elkesley Wood.
    Follow the main path as it meanders initially through broadleaf then
    amongst conifer trees to meet a major cross-track. Go left here (with the
    blue arrow) up a gentle incline. After about 100m, where the main track
    bears to the left, go right (with the Robin Hood Way sign and blue arrow)
    along a path which drops gently to emerge from the trees with Beggar's
    Rest cottage to the left.

3. Go forward on the track as it rises to a major lane crossing. (This is West
    Drayton Avenue, which links Clumber Park with the church at Milton,
    six miles to the east (see Walk 16). Here, in the 1830s, the Fourth Duke of
    Newcastle created a mausoleum for his wife and planted the link with
    lime trees and poplars. Sections of the avenue are now private property
    but there is still much which can be walked freely). Cross the lane and
    pass through a bridlegate beside metal field gate to follow a farm track as
    it swings right around the edge of Haughton Park House Farm. Where the
    Robin Hood Way (and Walk 24) swings to the left along the main access
    track, go straight on, passing the farmhouse with cupola to your right.
    We now follow a wide grassy (and sometimes muddy) lane, passing
    through two sets of metal field gates and with the tower of Bothamsall
    church in the distance ahead. More green lane and a bridlegate take us
    into the outskirts of the village and to the church.

    Bothamsall, originally an estate village of the Dukes of Newcastle, is grouped
    around a single street. The village name is certainly descriptive of its location
    since in Domesday Book it was spelt 'Bodmescel', meaning 'the shelf by a broad
    river valley'. The church of Our Lady and St Peter was built in the Perpendicular
    style in 1845 to replace a 14th-century original. It is a mass of battlements,
    pinnacles and gargoyles and is a beautifully compact building with spindly
    battlemented tower complete with corner pinnacles external stair turret and war
    memorial clock together with nicely proportioned nave, north aisle and chancel.
    Outside, nothing remains of the original building but internal stonework in the
    floor and the font can be dated to the 14th century.

4. Leave the church by dropping down steps at the west end beneath the
    tower, and onto Main Street. [Note: the plaque in the wall which informs
    us that Bothamsall won the Best-kept village title for three years in a row
    from 1986]. Go forward, signed to Thoresby and Warsop, following the
    road as it winds through and out of the village. [Walk 24 comes in from
    the left on Meadow Lane just before we lose the pavement]. Soon the

Walk 15 - Elkesley-Bothamsall-Crookford

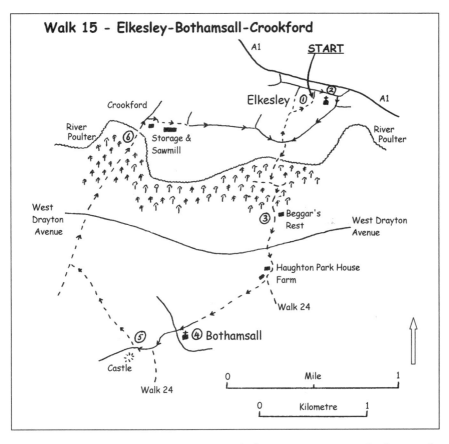

pavement is lost and great care is needed as we mount a gentle slope with a blind bend at the top. There is a fine ornamental village sign here with quarters showing the church, a wheatsheaf, an obvious cricket interest and the mound of Bothamsall Castle which can be seen over the road to the left. There is little information available about this fine mound but it is thought to have been a 12th-century motte and bailey fortification – ideally situated to command the surrounding area!

5. Turn right through hedge gap at the top of the slope, and, following the direction of the finger-pointer, walk diagonally left down the field, aiming to pass immediately to the left of a mid-field wooden power post. Continue to the field edge then go forward with ditch and hedge to your left to arrive on a farm track. Go right here to a surfaced lane (West Drayton Avenue again) then straight over to follow the line of power posts into and through a stretch of woodland. At the large woodland

Our Lady and St Peter, Bothamstall

glade, keep over to the right and follow the sandy track with trees to your right as far as the River Poulter ford (Crookford).

6. Cross by the bridge beside the ford and continue along the road for 100m then go right, passing a container storage area to your right and climbing gently on a surfaced lane. Follow the lane as it bends to the right then, immediately before entering the gates of a sawmill and storage area, go left onto a narrow path which runs alongside the perimeter fence with tree-line to your left. The path joins a surfaced lane at the rear entrance to the mill and here, continue forward along the lane which dips and rises to the outskirts of Elkesley. At the T-junction, where the main lane swings left, go right (on Brough Lane) and continue, initially with house gardens left. (There are good views of Bothamsall church tower far over to the right from here). A few metres before the point at which we turned down to Elkesley Wood at the start of the walk, go left onto a headland path with a hedge to your right. [Note: this is a Permissive Path through the Nature Conservation area – the definitive (and rarely walked) route begins opposite the outward path down to the Elkesley Wood]. Where the hedge ends, bear right to join the perimeter fence of the sports field. Continue with the perimeter fence to your immediate right and, where this ends, go right, crossing the top of a children's play area and the sports field then left, back into the car park.

16. Tuxford – East Markham – Milton – West Markham

Distance: 7½ miles (12km)

Maps: OS Landranger 120: Mansfield & Worksop, Sherwood Forest. OS Explorer 271: Newark-on-Trent; Retford, Southwell & Saxilby

Start: Public parking adjacent to the Sun Inn Car Park, Newark Road, Tuxford (GR 736709)

Churches: St Nicholas, Tuxford; St John the Baptist, East Markham; Newcastle Mausoleum, Milton; All Saints, West Markham

The Walk

Field paths and quiet roads take us to the magnificent Perpendicular church at East Markham, the rather severe Newcastle mausoleum at Milton and the lucky Norman survivor of West Markham. We return to Tuxford and its fine spire by green lanes with great distant views. This really is an experience of four totally different styles of church architecture.

Tuxford appears as 'Tuxfarne' in Domesday Book but, by the 12th century, we have Tukesford. The meaning is not entirely clear but it might be 'the ford of a man called Tuk' (an Old Scandinavian personal name with the Old English word ford). The town received its market charter in 1218 and five hundred years later, Daniel Defoe was describing it as "a dirty little market town" but this was probably before it was almost entirely rebuilt following a disastrous fire in 1702 which destroyed many of its older buildings. Tuxford gained its later importance as a major staging post at the junction of the Great North Road and the road from Lincoln to Ollerton. Now the Great North route bypasses the town and we can visit its pleasant market square and church in peace. Most prominent in the Market Place is the Newcastle Arms, a large Georgian hotel with, opposite, the stump of an old market cross. Hidden away but well worth seeking out on Newcastle Street, is the old town lock-up, which bears the date 1823. It was used to detain offenders until such time as they could be brought before a justice of the peace. Bearing in mind how busy Tuxford must have been as a coaching stop, it probably housed more than its fair share of drunks and pickpockets in its time.

The Route

1. Return to Newark Road and go left to the Market Place with the Sun Inn on the corner to your left and the Newcastle Arms beyond. Go right onto Lincoln Road and to the church.

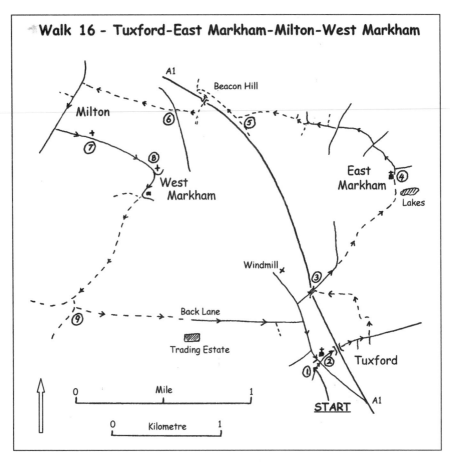

Walk 16 - Tuxford-East Markham-Milton-West Markham

St Nicholas, fortunately spared from the fire of 1702, sports a fine recessed spire on its battlemented tower. The nave, aisles and lower section of the tower date from the 13th century. The upper stages of the latter and the spire itself are of a hundred years later, while the clerestory comes from the 1470s. The chancel was rebuilt by the Prior of Newstead Abbey in 1495 and is lower than its predecessor, as can be seen by the original roof line on the east wall of the nave. Inside the building, the north arcade is of the 13th century while that to the south may date from around 1300. The font is of 1662, its cover bearing the date 1673. There are some interesting memorials inside the church, including one to William Dobson, an Excise Officer who died in 1761 but the gem here is the chapel to the north of the chancel which contains magnificent monuments and hatchments of the White family who were baronets of Wallingwells and formerly of Tuxford. These include one to Captain Charles White who served with Wellington in the Peninsula

Campaign and who was killed at Bayonne in 1814. Also here are two very worn 14th-century monuments. Note also the list of rectors and Vicars going back to William in 1179 and, set in the floor of the south aisle, gravestones dating from the mid 17th century. Opposite the church is the library, previously the grammar school, which was founded in 1669 by Charles Read of Darlton who made a fortune in shipping.

2. Return to the Lincoln Road and go left with the old school (now the library) over to your right. Pass beneath the A1 road bridge and continue past Ash Vale Road and opposite the next road (Faraday Avenue), go left over a finger-posted stile. Drop down the field, clipping the edge of a small copse to your right and continue to a stile beside field gate. Cross, and go left, along the headland, with ditch and hedge to your left (the definitive path goes straight over this field but the normally walked route is along the headland as described). A few metres on, the headland makes a little bump to the right and at this point, go right along a grassy division between fields, the path rising gently towards a lone tree on the skyline. At the field edge, go left along the track with a hedge to your right and follow it eventually round to the right to arrive on the Markham road with the A1 down to the left.

3. Go right along the road for about 300m and where it bends sharply to the left, go forward through a hedge gap and into a field corner. Cross two fields, aiming just to the right of the church tower, which can be seen in the distance. Cross the stile at the far field edge and continue down the gentle slope of the field, now aiming for the distant cooling towers Cottam Power Station, (those of High Marnham are to the right) to arrive at a field-edge footbridge. Cross the bridge and continue with a hedge left and fishing lake stretching away to your right. Cross the stile at the far side of the field and bear right, going gently up-slope and through a little gateway into the south grounds of the church.

The two Markhams of today shared the name 'Marcham' in Domesday Book but by 1192, the name 'Estmarcham' appears, the prefix added to distinguish it from its neighbour in the west. Later, during the Tudor period, East Markham became known as Great or Much Markham, suggesting that it had outgrown its neighbour. The village name reverted to 'East' at the end of the 18th century and it has been known as such since then. East Markham was a thriving market town but lost its prominence in 1609 when it was struck by the plaque, a catastrophe resulting in 114 local deaths, all of which were recorded by the local vicar who himself succumbed as the last, and 115th victim. It was probably this that caused the market to move to nearby Tuxford and East Markham now sits quietly and almost unseen, apart from its church, just to the south of the busy A57. The tower of St John the Baptist is a landmark for miles around and although looking very much like many other 15th-century churches of the area, this wonderful building really is something different. Proportionally it is perfect and restorations, particularly in the 1880s, have been in the greatest of taste. The oldest part of the church is the chancel arch, which dates from the 14th century. Of about the same time is the odd font base, although the bowl dates from 1686 and the great wooden cover is a couple of years later. The lovely screen was to have been replaced in 1897 but work was never completed due to a disagreement between the 7th Duke of Newcastle (who was to provide much of the funding), the vicar of the time and his churchwardens. The money allocated eventually went to Egmanton church instead. The many church monuments are for the ponderer and wanderer and would take pages to describe in detail. Sufficient then to mention the main ones and to let you find the others. There is a fine brass to Millicent Meryng who died in 1419 as the wife of Sir William Meryng. She had been twice married before, firstly to Sir Nicholas Burdon who was slain at the Battle of Shrewsbury in 1408 and secondly, to Judge Markham, by whom she bore a son, John, the future Lord Chief Justice. The most famous monument though is that to Sir John Markham himself. He died in 1409, and it was he who drew up the documents which resulted in the deposing of Richard II in favour of Henry IV (Bolingbroke). The chest containing the old judge is covered with graffiti – one example scratched as early as 1647, while others appear to be improvised gaming boards. This really is a church in which to spend time and to make use of the little booklet that is usually available for a small donation.

4. Leave the church by the north gate and go forward onto Church Street. At the junction with Mark Lane/Hall Lane, cross into Low Street. Continue to the next crossing (with Farm Lane) and go left then right into York Street. Continue along this quiet meandering lane for about 300m then, immediately after Richmond House to your left and where the lane makes a sharp bend to the right, go left onto a grassy path with garden hedges to either side. Emerging into a field corner, continue, initially with a hedge to your right and cross a narrow neck of arable land to a finger-post then go forward onto a grassy path which soon widens to a green lane and eventually arrives at a stile. Cross onto a field edge and continue your line, gently up-slope, aiming for a section of fence in the thick hedge ahead.

5. Cross the stile and go right, keeping close to the fence on your right and with the noise of the busy A1 down in the cutting to the left. Where the fence becomes a hedgeline, go right, over a stile, then immediately left, to continue the line of walk with a hedge to your left. At the field corner, (which is virtually the top of Beacon Hill – 75m above sea level!), cross a stile and drop down steps through scrub and trees and with magnificent views ahead, to a farm track. Go left, following the track as it swings left then sharply right to cross the bridge over the A1. On the far side, the definitive pathline goes right for a few metres then left, over the field to join a farm track. The preferred route though, is to follow the farm track forward from the A1 bridge then, at the track T-junction, go right and arrive on the (old) Great North Road (B1164) with the Mussel & Crab Restaurant and Bar opposite.

6. Cross the road with care and follow the finger-posted bridleway which runs along the left side of the bar/restaurant with distant views (when the leaves are off the trees) to the front left of the Milton mausoleum and, directly left, the little church at West Markham. Cross a bridleway bridge and continue forward on a track between open fields, eventually picking up a hedgeline to our right then to either side before dropping gently to a minor road. Go left into the hamlet of Milton and, after about 500m, go left at the first junction, climbing gently to the Newcastle mausoleum.

The Mausoleum was built as the last resting-place of Georgiana, wife of the Fourth Duke of Newcastle. The Duchess had fourteen children but died at the age of 34 giving birth to twins in 1822. It is said that she had expressed the wish to be buried on the hill here, which she could see from her residence at Clumber. The sad

Newcastle Mausoleum, Milton

fact is, that there was already an ancient but crumbling church just 800m away at West Markham but this was obviously not fine enough for the Duchess. The name of the parish was changed to Markham Clinton, Clinton being the family name of the Duke and he had the road linking Clumber to West Markham planted with alternate lime trees and poplars – the route we met in Walk 15 as West Drayton Avenue. License was given in 1824 to 'take down the Parish church of All Saints and rebuild it on a more convenient and elevated situation'. The structure we see today was designed by Sir Robert Smirke, who also designed the British Museum. It has a long nave, transepts and chancel and a tall octagonal and domed central tower. The intention was that the nave, entered by a plain west doorway, should be the parish church, while the transepts and chancel accessed by a grand eastern portico with four Doric columns should serve as the burial places of the family. The building was consecrated in 1833 by the Archbishop of York and remained the parish church until 1949, by which time, the 8th Duke had sold his estates. No further interest was taken in the mausoleum, most of the Newcastle family remains were moved to Clumber and the mausoleum declared redundant in 1971. By the greatest piece of good fortune, the lovely All Saints church was never demolished – it was just allowed to crumble – but now, thankfully, it has been lovingly restored and services are again held there.

7. Continue along the lane, dropping gently to the church of All Saints, West Markham.

This is a magnificent little church, lucky to survive the battle with the mausoleum at Milton but in its survival, it managed to miss the Victorian restoration that might otherwise have ravaged it. It has a remarkable wooden bell tower, stone nave with half-timbered west gable, chancel and half-timbered south porch. In the south wall of the nave, there is some herring-bone work, a section of which has been especially revealed on the inside. More such work can be seen above the south door, which is itself very ancient and set within a Norman doorway. Another Norman doorway can be found in the south wall of the chancel. The porch was added in the 16th century. Inside there is a magnificent tub font with crudely carved figures which is believed to date 'not later than 1090' and there are some fine old carved bosses in the more modern wooden beams in the roof. A list of rectors is displayed which goes back to Henry in 1179.

8. Return to the lane and go left, ignoring the side lane dropping down to the left, and follow the main route which swings gently to the right and mounts to bend sharply left beside barns. Here, go forward onto a surfaced lane signed as a cul-de-sac and continue to climb gently, leaving the last of the cottages behind as our route becomes a stony track with great views. Stay on this track for almost three-quarters of a mile. At the top of the long slope, ignore the greenway going off to the front and stay with the main route which bends to the left, ignoring another track going off to the right.

9. We are now on Back Lane which drops gently with views of the cooling towers of Cottam Power Station in the distance ahead with, to their right, the spire of Tuxford church. Our lane continues its downward way, with the scars of trading estates down to the right and becomes a metalled track with, soon, views of Longbottoms windmill to the front left. This four-storied brick and tarred structure dates from the 19th century. It has been restored with sails and fantail and, although no longer working, retains most of its machinery intact. Stay with the main lane as it drops to the old Great North Road (B1164) to go right, gently uphill into Tuxford market place, the Sun Inn and so back to our start point.

17. Dunham on Trent – Fledborough – Ragnall

Distance: 7 miles (11.3km)

Maps: OS Landranger 121: Lincoln & Newark on Trent. OS Explorer 271: Newark-on-Trent; Retford, Southwell & Saxilby

Start: Ample parking on the west (Dunham) bank of the River Trent adjacent to the A57 toll bridge (GR 818745).

Churches: St Gregory, Fledborough; St Leonard, Ragnall; St Oswald, Dunham

The Walk

A walk with a bit of everything – river bank, country lane and cross-field sections. There are three fine churches, one still very active, one almost forgotten in its isolation and another sadly neglected. Note that the last field on the approach to Fledborough along the Trent bank is sometimes used for grazing cattle. These are often inquisitive but in the past have never proved to be bellicose!

Dunham, spelt 'Duneham' in Domesday Book, and meaning 'the village or homestead at the hill', has two pubs, a lovely church and manages to retain its quiet village atmosphere despite lying astride the busy A57. To the east is the toll bridge, which crosses the River Trent and links Nottinghamshire and Lincolnshire. It stands on the site of the old ferry which was replaced by a four-arch cast iron bridge in the 1830s, itself to be replaced by the present structure in the 1970s. Immediately to the south is the pipe that carries water from Elkesley to Lincoln.

The Route

1. Pick up the Trent embankment path and follow it southwards with the river down to the left. (The definitive footpath keeps close to the bank of the river then passes between lakes before, at their southern end, swinging right to rejoin the main embankment). However, the normally walked route is along the embankment top, passing the lakes which are a haven for water birds and slowly drawing nearer to High Marnham Power Station which can be seen in the distance ahead. We eventually walk beside a wooden fence to our right with house over, before crossing a stile onto a dirt lane. Turn right, into Fledborough.

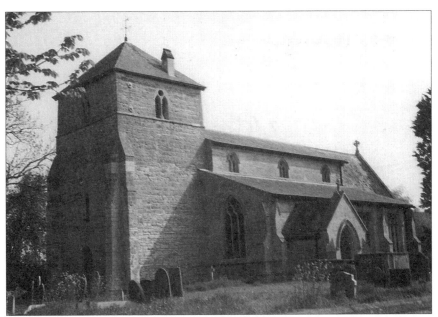

St Gregory, Fledborough

Fledborough seems much too tiny a place for such a lovely church. Documents as early as 1060 mention the village as 'Flatburche' but by 1080, it was 'Fladburh', coming from the Old English meaning 'the stronghold on the stream'. It is one of those places rarely found by the casual traveller but there may have been many such in the early 18th century when the local Rector set up a Gretna Green equivalent by announcing he would join in wedlock any who applied to him. The church of St Gregory is approached by a wooden gateway, which looks as though it might once have been part of the old church doorway. There is a magnificent, heavy and stumpy west tower, the lower stage of which dates from Norman times. Above, the structure is of the 13th century and is capped with a pyramid topping. The north and south aisles also date from this period (but note the sealed arch in the east wall of the south aisle), while the clerestory comes from the 14th century, although it was heavily restored in the latter half of the 19th. The 15th-century porch has an old sundial built into its wall and the church possesses some wonderful 14th-century glass.

2. Return to the lane and go right, with the towers of High Marnham Power Station soon towering over us to the left. The power station, with its five cooling towers each reaching 104m into the sky first began production in 1959 and was Britain's first 1000MW plant. We stay with the lane for almost three-quarters of a mile, ignoring finger-posted paths to the right

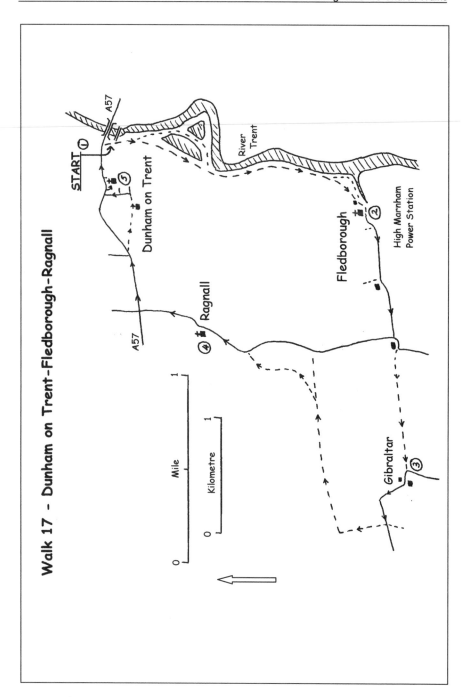

Walk 17 – Dunham on Trent–Fledborough–Ragnall

and eventually arrive on a minor road. Go forward along the road for about 100m and where it bends sharply to the left, bear right onto the finger-posted driveway of (Long Row) cottages. Where the drive swings to the right, go forward over a stile and continue along a headland path with fence to the right. Joining a farm track, we continue our line of walk with a hedge/ditch to our right and with occasional glimpses of the pyramid-capped tower of Darlton church far over to the front right. Where the main track bends off to the left, continue forward, with broken hedge to the right, eventually to cross a stile onto a country lane (Far Road).

3. Continue forward along the lane, passing between the isolated buildings which make up the settlement named as Gibraltar on mapping. Follow the road as it bends to the right, then more sharply to the left and follow it for a further 350m. Immediately beyond a thicket of bushes and trees to your right and a finger-posted footpath to the left, leave the road and go right onto a finger-posted bridleway. Stay with this headland route to the field corner to bear right over a bridleway bridge then sharply right onto a grassy track with a hedge/ditch to your right. Follow the bridleway now for about three-quarters of a mile, crossing two more bridges and picking up the Fledborough Beck down to your right. After the second of the bridges, continue forward along the beckside for a further 350m to pass through a gap in the hedge that comes down from the left. 200m on from here, at the next field corner (marked by a small dike, which comes in from the left), leave the main path and aim diagonally left across the field. [Note: This path is usually signed and defined but if this is not the case, please follow the description with care. If in difficulty, continue along the beckside to the road, then go left, along the road, to rejoin the route at the end of the cross-field section]. Cross the field, as directed by the finger-post, aiming for another finger-post which can be seen in the distance and which stands beside a footbridge. Cross the bridge and bear right, aiming now for a point immediately to the left of the red brick houses of Ragnall then, when it comes into view, the right-hand corner of a metal paling fence, which encloses a pumping station, where we emerge onto a road. Bear left along the road, entering the tiny village of Ragnall and, 500m on, the gateway into the churchyard.

Ragnall is a tiny village of a few houses, farms and a church. In Domesday Book, it is spelt 'Ragenehill' which comes from the Old Scandinavian meaning 'the hill of a man called Ragni'. The church of St Leonard is a sad little building with a population unable to maintain it as a place of worship. The battlemented west tower is of fine stonework and sports a tiny pyramid top and a clock permanently telling us that it is just past nine o'clock. The nave, the north wall of which has a sealed doorway, and the south aisle are of similar stone and the south doorway is guarded by two fine crowned heads. The chancel gives a more modern appearance; it was rebuilt in the 1860s when much of the remainder of the building was restored. Some of the windows are original and date from the 14th and 15th centuries, the east window being especially fine but, sadly, much of the interior of the building has been gutted.

4. Return to the road and go left, meandering gently up-slope to the A57. We need to go right here but the safe walkway is on the far side of the road so, cross the busy junction with the greatest of care. Go diagonally right and pick up a path on the far side, which is initially separated from the road itself by a wide band of grass and bushes. Walking close to the road edge now, cross the entrance to Upper Row (lane) and, 100m on, go right to recross the A57 with great care and pick up a finger-posted drive-way. Following the gravelled drive and as it swings left into the cottage garden, keep well over to the left, hugging the garden hedge and with the house and garage to your right. Cross the stile at the corner of the garden and continue over the field beyond to arrive at the end of a cul-de-sac (Leach Close/Horne Lane) in the village of Dunham. Walk down the lane then take the first left (The Green) which leads us to the A57 with the War Memorial cross on the corner to the right. Go right, then right again immediately before the Bridge Inn and follow the lane (Church Walk) as it swings left and continues through a beautiful and ancient stone arch-way surmounted by an ornate cross and into the church grounds.

The church of St Oswald is a wonderful building with a large and impressive battlemented and corner-pinnacled west tower, the upper stage of which has huge 15th-century windows open to the air. To the east is a very high and relatively narrow nave and, by comparison, a very low and almost insignificant chancel – both rebuilds of 1861-1862. This rebuild apparently heightened the roof of the nave and steepened its pitch since the original line can be seen in the east wall of the tower. Above the west door, which has an inscribed date of 1862, is the strange epitaph – 'How dreadful is this place'! There are some interesting gravestones in the churchyard including one in memory of Thomas Whitehead Junior, who died on 3rd October, 1770, aged 42. Thomas was apparently a traveller who had lodged at the village inn and died there, his inscription reading:

I that have lodg'd in many a Town, and travell'd far and near, till Death with his Dart, Struck me to the Heart, and now my lodging's here.

5. Leave the churchyard by the alley at the north-west corner, passing beneath another archway, which leads through a kissing gate and onto the A57 (Dunham Main Street). Go right to return to the toll bridge and the start point.

18. Harby – Thorney

Distance: 7¼ miles (11.5km)

Maps: OS Landranger 121: Lincoln & Newark-on-Trent. OS Explorer 271: Newark-on-Trent; Retford, Southwell & Saxilby

Start: All Saints church, Harby (GR 878705). Ample parking on the sports field opposite the church. Note that the field is sometimes used for car boot sales on Sundays during Spring and Summer and can be very busy at such times.

Churches: All Saints, Harby; St Helen, Thorney

The Walk

A lovely stroll close to the Lincolnshire border which takes us over and around fields, along country lanes and includes two fine churches. The initial section is repeated on the return journey, but walking it in reverse makes this hardly noticeable.

Harby appears as 'Herdrebi' in Domesday Book and has the probable meaning of 'the farmstead of Herrothr', the latter being an Old Scandinavian personal name. The village is best known for its association with an event which took place here two hundred years after Domesday Book: Queen Eleanor of Castille, the wife of Edward I, died at the Manor House in 1290, the ditches in the field near the church being the only reminders of Richard de Weston's home, where she spent her last days. Eleanor, a Spanish princess, married Edward when she was ten and he just fifteen years of age. Despite their youth, the couple were devoted to each other and she was his constant companion during his travels, even going on a crusade with him. Edward was on a campaign to subdue the Scots when Eleanor fell ill. She remained in Harby while Edward held court at Clipstone and visited the abbeys of Newstead and Rufford. The Queen finally died on 27th November, 1290 and Edward mourned her with the words "I loved her tenderly in her lifetime and I do not cease to love her now she is dead". After three days of mourning at Harby he accompanied her body to Lincoln where her internal organs were buried and her body embalmed. The funeral cortège then made its way by stages to London and, at every stopping place, the King ordered the erection of a cross dedicated to her memory, the final one being at Charing. The church of All Saints is a compact, aiseless, cruciform building which was reconstructed in 1875 in an Early English style. It has a fine broach spire and a clock tower which contains a miniature effigy of Queen Eleanor with the date 1290 (a modern inscription). At the Queen's sides are her coats of arms – England far left, Ponthieu far right and Castille and Leon between. In the porch, a notice proclaims 'The Incorporated Society for building and churches granted £100, AD 1874 towards rebuilding the church upon condition that all the seats be for the free use of the parishioners according to law'. Inside there is a fine painted cloth showing the route of Queen Eleanor's cortège from Harby to London; a brass plate on the floor just before the altar rail tells us that 'Here died Aleanor of Castille, Queen of England, 27th November, 1290'.

The Route

1. Return to Church Road and go left, passing the sports field over to your right. Ignore the finger-posted bridleway to the right and continue to the village centre, going forward (along High Street), passing the village hall (no parking) to your left then The Bottle & Glass inn to your right. The road bends to the left to arrive at a T-junction where we go right onto Station Road, signed to Lincoln. 150m on, having passed beside farm buildings but immediately before bungalows, go left over a finger-posted double stile and onto a path that leads beside a garden fence to your right. At the end of the fence, continue to pass a power post to your right and arrive at an unmarked field edge. Bear diagonally right here, over the field, to a stile and sleeper bridge. Cross, and bear left to continue the original line of walk over the next field, aiming for the top field corner. Here, cross another sleeper bridge and stile onto a farm track. Go left with the track for a few metres then right. A few metres on, where a hedge comes in from the left, go left along the headland with ditch and hedge to your right. 50m on, go right over a sleeper bridge and stile. Bear gently left over the field to a stile in the far hedgeline which takes us into another field where we continue the line to a stile beside a metal gateway and onto a dismantled railway line.

2. Cross, and pass between concrete posts to bear left over the next field and arrive at a large footbridge over a deep drain (Ox Pasture Drain). Cross the bridge and go half left (*not sharply left along the drain*) to pick up a headland path with stunted treeline to your left and with the cooling towers of High Marnham in the distance ahead. At the field corner, go right on a wide path, picking up a ditch down to your left. At the next field corner, go left, crossing a culvert then walking a farm track, which takes us towards woodland ahead. Follow the track as it swings to the right, with trees on the left, to reach a country road (Brown Lane).

3. Go right here and, ignoring the road left signed to Thorney, pass farm

buildings to your left and as the road bends to the right, go left through the finger-posted gateway of The Hollies. Where the main track swings right to the house, go forward along a grassy way, crossing a stile and picking up a headland path with ditch and treeline to your right. Cross the stile beside gate at the field corner and continue forward with trees to your right. We walk along the edge of the wall perimeter of Thorney Hall to our right then fishing ponds to the left to cross a stile onto road (Top Road). Go right, passing the gateway to Thorney Hall, enter the tiny village and so arrive at the church.

Thorney is given as 'Torneshaie' in Domesday Book and comes from the Old English meaning 'the thorn tree enclosure'. Since the 16th century, Thorney has been closely linked with the Nevile family but, long before that, in about 1202, records show that the patronage of the church was given by Walter de Clifford to the Prioress of Broadholme (now a tiny churchless parish which was incorporated into Lincolnshire in 1989).

By 1544 the patronage had passed to Edward Fynes and Robert Tirwhit but in 1567 the estate was purchased by George Nevile of Ragnall and it remained with that family on and off until the 1960s. In the early 18th century, the Neviles built a magnificent mansion in the grounds to the south of the present church and it was the building of this church in 1849/1850, which, amongst other things, broke the family finances. By the 1890s, the demise of the Nevile family in Thorney was almost complete and during the First World War, the Hall was used as a convalescent home. Following the war, the Neviles bought back the

St Helen, Thorney

Hall but most of the land was sold to local farmers. Various members of the family lived here between 1918 and 1962 but the Neviles finally left and in 1964 the old Hall was demolished and replaced by a modern building. The church of St Helen presents a magnificent west front with its mock Norman doorway, three lancets above and a beautiful circular window topped off with an incredibly ornate double bellcote. The whole building is a marvellous mass of modern Norman and Romanesque – bursting with gargoyles and carvings, which resemble African masks – there is even an ornate dovecote, which disguises the vestry chimney. Just inside the west door are two fonts – the magnificently carved Norman original and an almost equally impressive modern version. The aisle walls are decorated with fine Nevile hatchments while, at the east end of the nave, are the magnificent modern carved pulpit and lectern – copies of the originals. Outside in the churchyard to the east are remains of the earlier church in the form of beautiful 15th-century windows and arches. Also here are some tombs of the Neviles. Of much more recent history, there are five graves to members of the Royal Air Force, four of whom sadly lost their lives on the same day – 31st August, 1944.

4. Returning to the road, go right for about 100m then right again onto a finger-posted gravel driveway with wall to the right and garden hedges left. Where the driveway swings to the right, go straight on over a stile beside gateway and follow a narrow path between hedge and fence. A waymarker takes us to the left and along the edge of woodland and on to a stile to the right. Cross, going right, and follow a grassy path with the woodland still to the right to another stile which we cross then go left along the field headland with fence then hedge to our left. Continue through a gap in the field corner then go right with ditch and trees to the right. Pass through a wide gap in the hedge that comes in from the left and go left, with the hedge and trees to the left and soon, paddock fence to the right. At the field corner, go forward over a plank bridge then right on a farm track which leads to Springwood Farm.

5. Walk between the farm building to your right and garage left and, passing through a gateway, go left, *not along the farm track but along a headland path* with trees and ditch to your left and open field to the right. Pass through the gap at the field corner and go right with hedge and trees to your right. Go through the gap at the next field corner and continue forward with ditch and hedge to your right for 200m then go left across the field (there is usually a waymarker to show the point of departure from the headland) at right angles to the previous path. At the far side of the field, go right with ditch and treeline to your left and, passing a poultry farm over to the left, emerge onto a country lane (Drisney Nook Lane).

Walk 18 - Harby-Thorney

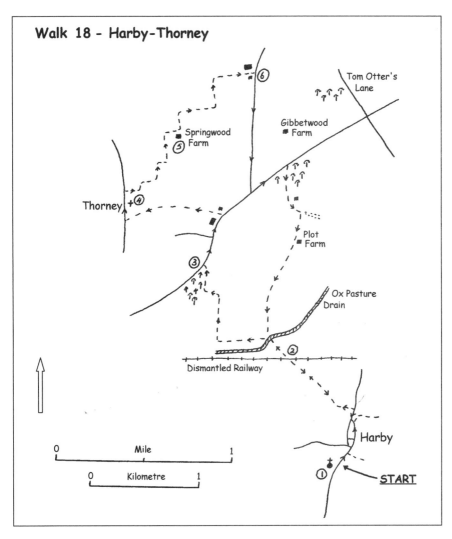

6. Go right along the lane, soon passing the entrance to Gibbetwood Farm to your left. (The name refers to the woodland which lies to the north of the farm and which takes its name from an incident that took place near here on 3rd November, 1805. It is said that a worker by the name of Thomas Temporell, but known as Tom Otter, was forced to marry a girl from South Hykeham (Lincoln) after he had made her pregnant. He was not particularly happy about the accusation or the marriage and murdered her on their wedding night, leaving the body on the steps of the Sun Inn in nearby Saxilby. Otter was subsequently sentenced to death and was hanged outside Lincoln Castle on 14th March 1806. Six days later, his body was removed and gibbeted near the wood that bears the grisly name). Stay with the lane all the way to the T-junction where we go left, signed to Saxilby and Lincoln and 400m on, go right, with the finger-post, into a patch of woodland. (Straight on along the road would take us past Gibbet Wood and onto Tom Otter's Lane). Continue through the trees to a cross path then go right, as waymarked. Our path meanders slightly and emerges from the trees onto a field edge. Bear left over the field, passing derelict barns to your left and arrive on a farm track. Go left with hedge and trees to your right and follow the main track as it bends to the right (a lesser track continues onwards) with a hedge to the right and farm buildings ahead. We pass through the yard of Plot Farm and bear gently to the right along a track, which brings us out onto a field edge. Continue forward over this huge field. [Note that the path across this field is not always clearly defined – if this is the case, take the line of least resistance and with minimum damage to any crop until you catch sight of the waymarker at the far field edge which should then become your aiming mark]. At the far hedgeline, go forward through the gap and onto a headland path with a hedge to your right. The spire of Harby church in the distance is to the front left and, just in the foreground, the stump of Harby windmill tower. At the field corner, go right through the gap and arrive at the footbridge (over Ox Pasture Drain) which we crossed earlier in our walk. Go left over the bridge and retrace your steps to the start point in Harby.

19. Clifton – River Trent – Girton

Distance: 8 miles (13km)

Maps: OS Landranger 121: Lincoln & Newark-on-Trent. OS Explorer 271: Newark-on-Trent; Retford, Southwell & Saxilby

Start: St George's church, Clifton (GR 819712). The church is located at the roadside between North and South Clifton. There is ample parking in the layby outside the building or on adjacent roadside verges.

Churches: St George, Clifton; St Cecilia, Girton

The Walk

A pleasant stroll along the Trent bank followed by some cross-field paths which take us into the tiny village of Girton. Our return is by green lane and more field paths before country roads take us through the village of South Clifton and back to the start point. Much of the walk follows the route of the Trent Valley Way however, the cross-field sections do tend to get overgrown in summer months and it is therefore recommended that it be undertaken outside of this season.

Our walk begins at the church of St George which is shared by the villages of North and South Clifton and which is conveniently situated half-way between the two. Only the name 'Cliftone' appears in Domesday Book but by around 1160 we have a Nort Clifton and in 1280, Suth Clifton, the suffix being a common Old English place name meaning 'the farmstead on or near a cliff or bank'. Both villages sit close beside the Trent and near to the border with Lincolnshire but are entirely separate entities. North Clifton is perhaps best known as the site of a Meditation Centre and Japanese Garden. South Clifton, once a busy wharf where coal from Yorkshire and Derbyshire was unloaded, is today best known to English rugby union fans as the home of Dusty Hare who broke the world record for points scored in the sport in April 1981 and who was awarded the MBE in January 1989. The church is magnificently isolated, the backdrop of High Marnham Power Station if anything, amplifying the beauty of this Medieval monument. The grounds are entered through a large, 19th-century iron gateway announcing 'I am the Resurrection & the Life' on one side and 'I know that my Redeemer liveth' on the other. This looks a typical Nottingham-style Perpendicular church of battlemented tower with corner and intervening crocketed pinnacles (and some magnificent gargoyles), nave, chancel, north aisle and south porch. The lower stages of the tower though are quite early and come from around

1300. Inside, the arches to the nave and chancel date from the 12th or early 13th centuries and fine Norman pillars support the north arcade.

The Route

1. Take the footpath, which leaves the churchyard at the west (tower) end, crossing a stile into the graveyard extension then another stile into a field. Bear slightly to the right, down the field, to a wide gap between trees then right again to the field corner. Here, go left along the headland with the hedge and ditch over to your right, passing beneath power cables and at the field corner, go right over a stile beside fieldgate. Keeping hedge and ditch to your left, climb the embankment of the River Trent. (The viaduct that once carried the Mansfield to Lincoln railway is down to the right). Go left along the embankment, through a double gateway, with the river to your right to pick up the route of the Trent Valley Way. We stay with the embankment now for about 3½ miles, passing the suspended footbridge that links our bank of the river with the High Marnham Power Station on the far side, getting sight of the hamlet of High Marnham on the far bank, then the church of Low Marnham. Just beyond the 60km post, we pass beneath power cables and need to leave the river for a short distance, following the path with hedge to our left before picking up the embankment again. We pass the 59km and 58km posts, slowly approaching gravel workings ahead. The path is well-marked around the gravel works which crosses a footbridge over a conveyor belt and onwards to the works' access road with distant views to the front of Newark church spire and, over to the right, the tower of Sutton church.

2. [Note that the cross-field section onwards from here to Girton can be very overgrown in summer months. If you wish to avoid any possible difficulty, follow the wide hard earth/stone access road (which improves to a surfaced lane) for about half a mile then, immediately before a huge power pylon to your right, go right onto a green lane, soon reaching the stile which marks the end of the cross-field section to your right]. If following the cross-field route – where the road bends to the left, go straight on, over a finger-posted stile and bear left, keeping to the embankment which runs away from the river, soon picking up a hedge to your left. Cross the stile at the field corner and continue with hedge/trees now to your right. At the next field corner cross another stile (located down to the right) and continue with ditch and hedge/bushes to the right. Stay with the headland, passing an old brick furnace to arrive at a stile onto a dirt track. Go straight over, crossing another stile and

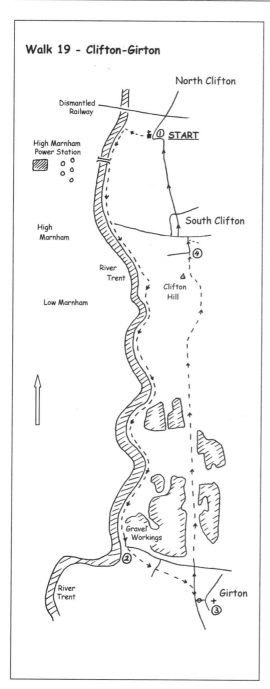

Walk 19 - Clifton-Girton

North Clifton

Dismantled
Railway

High Marnham
Power Station

① START

High
Marnham

South Clifton

River
Trent

④

Clifton
Hill

Low Marnham

Gravel
Workings

②

River
Trent

Girton

③

continue along an embankment to a stile in the far hedge, which we cross then stay with the embankment to another stile into a meadow. Cross and bear gently to the right to pass beneath power cables and arrive at a stile in the far hedgeline. Cross onto a lane and go right for 100m to a grass triangle then left on a narrow surfaced lane (West Lane) between cottages and into Girton. This leads to a road (High Street) with the village church opposite.

The tiny village of Girton lies between the meandering River Trent and the busy A1133 and was frequently subject to flooding up until the 1970s. In Domesday Book, the name is given as 'Gretone', coming from the Old English meaning 'the farmstead/village on gravelly ground' an apt title considering the mass of gravel workings to be found in the area. Several of these workings have now been flooded and provide facilities for those who enjoy fishing and boating. The lovely, simple, little church of St Cecilia was built in 1879, replacing a much older structure, possibly dating from the 13th century, and consists of a simple nave and chancel, a bellcote being positioned between the two, and a south porch. The west wall has a fine set of lancets with a circular

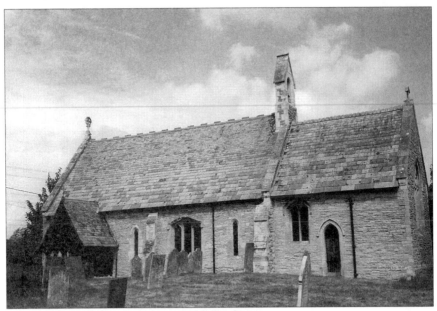

St Cecilia, Girton

window above. There is a lovely three-light east window, but the treasure here is the small 8th-century cross, which is set into the wall immediately to the right of the south doorway.

3. Leave the church and retrace your steps down West Lane to the grass triangle and go right, passing the stile by which we arrived to our left. Walk on along the green lane, crossing a narrow road and continuing forward for about a mile and a half in a straight line running almost due north. This is part of the Trent Valley Way and is not as boring as it might seem, for we pass the reclaimed gravel pits to either side and soon, conveyor belts carrying gravel from the workings. Our lane eventually becomes a grassy track, which leads into a field where we continue forward along the headland with a hedge to our left. At the field corner, cross a stile and plank bridge then, climbing the far embankment, continue over the next field where we mount a low bank and cross a stile to bear left, picking up the headland and keeping trees and hedges over to our left. Our route meanders with the headland to a concrete foot-bridge in the field corner, which crosses a very deep beck. Cross and bear gently to the right along a low embankment to a waymarker, which takes us diagonally left, up-slope, to join a farm track. Go left with the track (the triangulation point of Clifton Hill – 23m above sea level – is ahead) then almost immediately right, over the brow of the slope. As the track swings to the right, pause and admire the magnificent view which takes in Clifton and Low Marnham churches and the cooling towers of Cottam and High Marnham, as well as all the surrounding countryside of the Trent Valley. On a clear day, you can even see the towers of Lincoln Cathedral far over to the right. Our route now drops gently into the outskirts of South Clifton.

4. Continue forward on the surfaced lane, ignoring the finger-posted foot-path to the right and, at the junction of lanes, go left (along Vicarage Road), then right down Front Street with, on the left, the green with its oak tree and plaque to Dusty Hare. At the cross roads, go straight on, signed to North Clifton, and stay with this quiet road with wide grass verges as it leaves the village, bending to the left at the school building, then right and back to our start point.

20. Normanton on Trent – Weston – Sutton on Trent

Distance: 8¾ miles (14km)

Maps: OS Landranger 120: Mansfield & Worksop, Sherwood Forest, 121: Lincoln & Newark on Trent. OS Explorer 271: Newark-on-Trent; Retford, Southwell & Saxilby

Start: Ample parking at the Village Hall, Normanton, on the east side of South Street, opposite to the church (GR 791690). If more than a couple of cars are to use this facility, it would be polite to inform the keyholder. In the event that the hall car park is closed, there is limited roadside parking beside the south gateway of the church (on South Street).

Churches: St Matthew, Normanton; All Saints, Weston; All Saints, Sutton on Trent

The Walk

Country lanes, tracks and fieldpaths link three fine churches in this walk. Unfortunately, many of the cross-field and headland paths can become very overgrown during the summer months and it is therefore recommended that the walk be undertaken outside of that season. Also, cattle often graze a couple of fields near the start and one towards the end but these have always proved of the more friendly and unassuming type.

Normanton does not appear in Domesday Book but is a fairly common village name, coming from the Old English meaning 'the farmstead of the Northmen/Norwegian Vikings'. There is nothing outstanding about the church of St Matthew but it is neat and tidy and admirably suits the attractive village it stands in. It has a very plain exterior with none of the usual battlements or pinnacles. Rebuilding is evident, as can be seen by the mark left from the ridge of the old nave roof on the east wall of the tower. The nave arcades and chancel arch can be dated to the 13th or 14th centuries though the tower and clerestory are from the 15th. Opposite the church and close to the Village Hall car park entrance is a fine cottage with an interesting plaque which indicates that it was a school endowed with £4 a year for the education of 10 poor children of the parish in 1776.

The Route

1. Leave the church by the north-east gateway and go left onto East

Gate/Tuxford Road. Passing Mill Lane to your right, continue to the end of the brick perimeter wall to your left then, a few metres on, go left over a finger-posted stile in the hedgeline. Walk diagonally right over the field, passing to the right of horse chestnut trees and cross a stile and plank bridge into the next field corner. Continue the line, diagonally right over this field, aiming for the mid-point between two large trees in the far hedge. Cross the stile here and continue forward to the far field corner where a section of wooden fence with stile beside a huge tree stump leads into the next field. Continue the line again to the far field corner where another section of fence can be seen with, in the distance and to the right, the spire of Weston church. Pass beneath power cables and cross a stile onto the end of a gated green lane.

2. Go forward along the headland, keeping the hedge to your left and at the bottom of the field go right, still with the headland to reach a stile in the field corner. Cross this and the footbridge beyond and continue over the next field, aiming for the left-hand leg of the power pylon in the middle of the field. Pass beside the pylon and continue over a waymarked plank bridge to the field edge and a farm track. Go right along the track with a hedge and deep ditch to your left and, ignoring the footbridge to the left, arrive at a track junction and four-way finger-post. Go straight on along a tractor track that leads through a gateway and beside farm buildings then, the surface improving, arrive on the Weston-Normanton road. Go left, signed to Weston, passing beneath the railway arch and, at the end of the red brick farm outbuildings to your left, bear left over grass then a farm access drive to cross a brick parapet bridge and onto a field edge with a lovely view of the church at the top of the slope ahead. Bear slightly right over the field, aiming for an external hedge corner and here, go forward with the hedge to your right and the church ahead. Our path takes us through a kissing gate then onwards and gently upwards between hedges. At the top of the slope, go left with garden fence to the right and so to the base of the church tower.

Weston, set beside the Great North Road and thus once busy with coach traffic and well supplied with inns, is now a quiet little village and despite the suffix 'on-Trent', lies a good distance from the river. In Domesday Book, the name is given as 'Westone', coming from the Old English meaning 'west farmstead or village'. The church of All Saints is a little classic with battlemented tower supporting a fine recessed spire. There is a rather plain but tall south porch; the aisles are also plain but the clerestory and chancel are embattled, crocketed pinnacles having been added to the former. In the east wall of the tower can be seen the original roof line of the nave which previously reached the bell stage. The lower stages of the tower date from the 13th century, but the upper stage and the spire are a hundred years later. Inside, the arcades have octagonal pillars and are probably late 13th century and there is a fine 12th-century plain tub font. The south porch is approached along a yew tree avenue and leaving the church by this, note the headstone to the right with an inscription in memory of John Morris who died on 17th February 1749. He is said to have expired while chasing a local coach which he had just missed. The inscription reads: I nimble footman, once would outrun death, I ran so fast until I lost my breath, Death overtook me and made me his slave, And sent me with an errand to my grave.

3. Walk the pathway from the south porch and go right along Main Street. Continue through the village, eventually passing the converted Methodist Hall with a foundation stone dated 1877 to arrive at a triangle-road junction (with The old Great North Road). Cross the road and go left, up slope, for a few metres, then right onto a surfaced lane with The Boot & Shoe Hotel and Restaurant to your right. Follow the *main* lane, initially with hedge to your left, as it passes through an S-bend beside large storage sheds and 'nodding donkeys'. Our route soon becomes a dirt track and takes us over the A1. On the far side of the bridge, go right then left and, staying with the main track (ignore finger-posted path to the right), continue gently downwards between hedges. The lane swings to the right, then left along what is now a headland path with a hedge to the right, taking us through a hedge gap at a field corner where we go right then left, with a ditch now to our right. Over the field to the left is a patch of woodland (Wadnal Plantation). When we reach a point opposite the bottom end of the trees, we arrive at a (frequently overgrown) cross-track where we need to go left with ditch and intermittent trees to our right. Our path takes us to the bottom corner of the woodland where we cross a bridleway bridge and continue through the edge of the trees. Emerging from the woodland, a waymarker takes us to the left on a headland path with hedge to the left and on to the corner of another plantation (Cocked Hat Plantation). We follow the path round to the right (woodland to our left) to a cross-track and four-way finger-post.

4. Go straight over the junction, passing through a narrow hedge gap to pick up a headland path with a hedge to your left. Pass through a hedge gap at the field corner and continue forward, keeping hedgeline/trees to the left, to arrive on a country lane. Go straight on, (an access lane to Crow Park Farm goes off to the left here), down the lane for about 300m then go right through a bridlegate beside metal half-gate. Follow the farm track which drops then rises through sharp bends, eventually passing a plantation to your left (Lady Charlotte's Plantation). Ignore the waymarked footpath left at the end of the wood and continue forward, down-slope, with distant views of the spire of Carlton church to the front

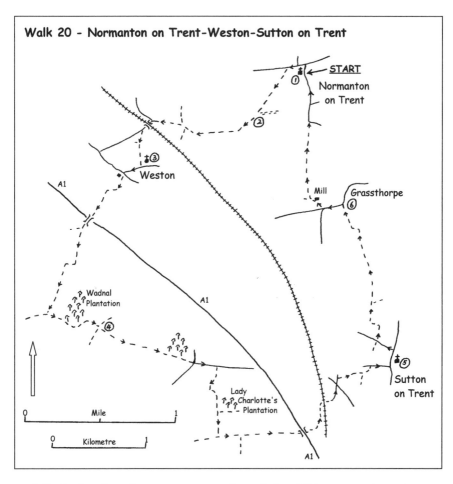

left. At the slope-bottom cross-track, go left, picking up a plantation to your right. Stay on this long straight section of track, which improves to a surfaced lane and, ignoring a waymarked lane to the right, continue all the way to the A1 embankment. Follow the lane as it bends to the right for a few metres then go left, walking beneath the road arch. Then, bear slightly right with the main lane, which soon swings to the left with the railway line running parallel to the right. 100m on, go right, through the wicket gates which lead over the railway at Eaves Lane Crossing. Stay with the lane as it bends left, passes farm buildings then swings to the right. At the first junction, go left along another lane (Barrel Hill Road) which leads to the busy B1164. Go straight over and continue down Hemplands Lane for 50m then, immediately after the first house to the right, go right onto a headland path with a hedge to your left. Stay with the headland which keeps beside garden hedges to arrive at a stile which we cross onto a field edge. Bear left over the field to the far corner to cross another stile and enter a passage between garden fences/hedges and onto a road (High Street). Go right, passing The Old England Hotel to the left and, at the T-junction, go left onto Church Street and so to the church.

Sutton on Trent, tucked away in the flatlands of the Trent bank, boasts a magnificent church and, at the south end of the village, a windmill dating from around 1814 which has a cupola but lacks fantail and sails. In Domesday Book, it appears as 'Sudtone', a common place name, which comes from the Old English meaning 'south farmstead or village'. All Saints bristles with battlements and crocketed pinnacles and is a model of well-proportioned ornateness, the only oddity being the south porch which seems a little out of place with its leaded roof and oddly shaped entrance. What we see here though is not quite all it seems, for this is a very heavily restored building. The lovely tower with its 13th-century look and 15th-century topping was rebuilt in 1902 (when Saxon foundations were unearthed – an old spire, removed in 1830, was not replaced) and much of the remainder was restored thirty years later. All of this was accomplished with such taste and sensitivity that even the odd porch was rebuilt with the original 'unfinished' look. There is so much here to draw the eye but especially noteworthy is the splendid Mering Chapel at the south-east corner. This encloses the marble tomb of Sir William Mering, of a family long extinct and whose lands have become the parish of the flood plain on the east bank of the Trent (we found traces of the family at East Markham). The chapel dates from around 1537; it abounds with pinnacled battlements and is finished with a magnificent frieze of shields, flowers and gargoyles. This is one of those churches to be admired from a shady tree in the yard as a late lunch is consumed.

5.   Leave the church by the west gate and go right along Church Street. Pass the school to your left then bear left onto Bulham Lane (Ingram Lane goes straight on). Immediately beyond the last house on the right (Treetops), go right onto a finger-posted path over grass and continue forward along a field headland with a hedge to your left. At the external field corner, go left, staying with the headland to arrive at a dirt track. Go right along the track and continue between open fields, eventually joining a stunted hedge to your right. At the field corner, continue the line, as directed by the finger-post, to arrive at a small footbridge with stile at either end. Cross and bear slightly left, aiming for a gap in the far hedgeline, crossing a grass airstrip and arriving at a stile. Cross this and continue forward over the next field slowly departing from the hedge to your right and aiming for a lone house which can be seen in the distance ahead to arrive at a wide hedge gap and culvert. Cross this and bear left, cutting the field

All Saints, Sutton on Trent

corner, to arrive at a hedgeline. Go right along the headland with hedge left to emerge onto a country lane in the tiny hamlet of Grassthorpe.

6. Go left for a couple of hundred metres then, where the lane swings sharply to the left and a track continues forward to the railway crossing, go right along a surfaced drive which leads to Grassthorpe Mill. Entering the garden, please take the greatest of care to stay on the right of way, which goes forward (house over to your right) and arrives at a stile in the fenceline. Do not cross this stile but go right, with the fence left, to the banks of a stream. Go right here with the stream down to your left then cross it by going left over a footbridge and cross a stile into a field. Go forward over the field, picking up a hedge to your right to arrive in the field corner. Cross the stile and continue over the next field, aiming towards the houses of Normanton, which can be seen in the distance. The path leads to an external field corner and a grassy lane where we pick up garden hedges to either side and emerge onto South Street, Normanton. Go straight on through the village, passing the (old Wesleyan) Methodist church with the date 1896 then The Crown inn and finally Elizabeth Hall cottages which are dated 1790, and so back to our start point.

21. South Collingham – Besthorpe – South Scarle – North Collingham

Distance: 9½ miles (15km)

Maps: OS Landranger 121: Lincoln & Newark-on-Trent. OS Explorer 271: Newark on Trent; Retford, Southwell & Saxilby

Start: Library/Medical Centre/shopping car park, east side of High Street, Collingham (GR 830617) where there is ample parking.

Churches: St John the Baptist, South Collingham; Holy Trinity, Besthorpe; St Helen, South Scarle; All Saints, North Collingham

The Walk

A stroll along country lanes, around fields and along a short section of the River Trent, taking in four churches, two of them in the same village. We also visit east Nottingham's 'Lake District' and wander for short distances along the Trent Valley Way. Although this walk might be undertaken at any time of the year, some of the field paths do tend to be overgrown in the summer months so that it might be advisable to avoid that particular season.

Collingham proudly boasts two fine churches, there once having been two separate settlements here with a Vicar at North Collingham and a Rector at South Collingham but since the 1970s, the two have been combined. There are some fine old buildings in the village, a couple of excellent inns and the stump of an ancient market cross. Up until the early 17th century when the River Trent retreated westwards, the village was frequently subjected to flooding and even in 1795 the houses were under 5ft of water! Marks outside the church at North Collingham indicate more recent high levels.

The Route

1. Return to High Street and go left (crossing the road as quickly as possible), passing The Royal Oak inn over to the left then going straight over the traffic light-controlled junction. Passing Lunn Lane to your right then The Kings Head inn and Dykes End to the left, leave the main road to bear right by a little green. Ignore the road signed to the River Trent and continue forward towards the church tower ahead. Follow the road as it bends to the left and then go right down Westfield Lane (also signed

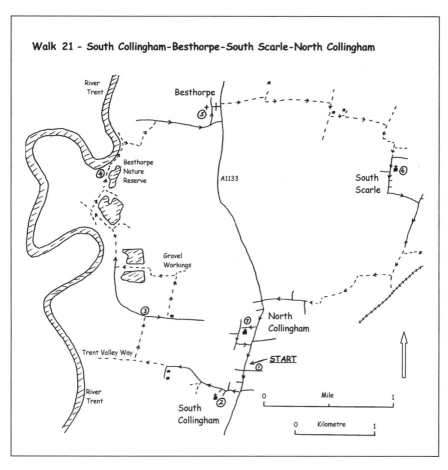

Walk 21 - South Collingham-Besthorpe-South Scarle-North Collingham

for the River Trent). 100m on, go left onto a driveway between houses which leads to the church of South Collingham.

At first sight, St John the Baptist appears a typical Nottinghamshire Perpendicular-style building, but outside appearances can be deceptive. The tall buttressed tower topped with battlements and large corner crocketed pinnacles is of two totally different periods, as can be seen by the stonework. The upper stage is of the 15th century, while the lovely old stones below are 13th-century work. In the east wall of the tower can be seen the earlier roof line of the nave which was lowered when the clerestory was added in the 15th century. The north arcade is the oldest part of the church and has wonderful Norman arches, one with an amazing corbel depicting a dragon-like creature with a bearded man's face. There is a very plain octagonal font, which dates from about 1250, and, set into the east wall of the north aisle is a memorial to Francis Mering with the date 1573. The lovely modern rood screen was erected in 1940. The list of Rectors not surprisingly begins with the same individual we shall find at North Collingham – Dominus Egidius de Erdyngton but he is followed here by Richard de Rowell (1268) and John de Drachs (1298).

2. Return to Westfield Lane and go left, now joining the Trent Valley Way. Cross a beck (The Fleet) and follow the lane as it bears to the right then left to pass beneath power cables. Where the main lane swings left to farm buildings, continue forward on what is now a dirt track signed to the River Trent. About 500m on, the track makes a slight bend to the right and here we go sharply right (leaving the Trent Valley Way) onto a green lane with hedges to either side which leads us to a field corner. Continue forward along what is now a headland track with hedge/trees to the right, eventually arriving on a surfaced lane (Carlton Ferry Lane).

3. Go right along the lane for about 300m and immediately before the lone cottage to your left, go left onto a finger-posted track with, initially, the red brick wall of an outhouse to your right. Soon we are walking a green lane between hedges with intermittent views of the spire of Carlton on Trent church to the far left. Just before the point where the lane swings right to pass beneath power cables and before reaching the perimeter fence of gravel workings, go left beside a lone tree to follow a headland path with a hedge to your right. At the field corner, go forward over a footbridge then right, as waymarked, with a hedge over to your right and lake to your left. At the end of this lake, go left, to pick up a pathway, which now runs between lakes to either side. At the lake end, go forward over grass to a stile onto a surfaced track (Carlton Ferry Lane again). Go right along the lane which eventually bends gently to the left with now, another lake over the hedge to your right. At the northern end of this lake and just beyond a finger-posted footpath to the left, go right onto a stony track with hedges to either side and the lake over to your right. Where the main track swings sharply to the right, go forward over a stile into Besthorpe Nature Reserve. (The reserve is separated from our path by a fence, which should not be crossed since the area is a habitat and nesting area for a large variety of birds and small animals). Continue forward, eventually bending with the path to the left and mounting the embankment of the River Trent.

4. Go right along the embankment with the river down to your left, crossing a culvert and following the river as it bends to the left. Just before the 53 kilometre post and a gateway across our route, go right, down the embankment and leaving the river behind, follow a headland path with a

hedge to the left. At the field corner, go left along a farm track with thick hedge/treeline to your right. The track bends to the right and eventually arrives at a gravel track (Trent Lane). Go right along the track which improves to a surfaced lane, passes beneath power cables and eventually bears left to enter the outskirts of Besthorpe village. Where the main lane swings to the right, go forward onto Low Road, into the 30mph speed restriction area and so to the tiny church.

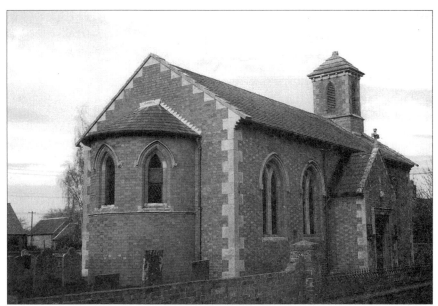

Holy Trinity, Besthorpe

Holy Trinity looks very much a structure of the modern times although it was, in fact, constructed in 1844 (at a cost of some £400). It is a tiny box building of red brick and white stone on an unusual north-south axis. The shallow porch is to the east while, at the northern end there is a strange rectangular bell turret with pyramid top and to the south, a rounded apsidal attachment. The only real indications of the age of the building are the 19th-century stones in the graveyard. Besthorpe does not appear in the Domesday Book but between 1147 and 1163, the name 'Bestorp' appears in written records. The meaning is not entirely clear but could be either 'the outlying farmstead/hamlet of Bosi' (an Old Scandinavian personal name) or 'the outlying farmstead/hamlet where the bent grass grows'.

5. From the church porch, go forward over the miniature green with the converted Methodist Chapel (1832) over to your right. Go straight over the mini cross-roads (rejoining the Trent Valley Way) and onto a major road crossing (with the A1133). Cross the road with care and go left for about 30m then, before The Lord Nelson inn over the road to the left, go right over a stile beside fieldgate (not the adjacent access drive). Go forward with the headland track with fence/trees to your left. We stay on this line now for about 600m, crossing a number of stiles beside gateways and arrive at a major track crossing. Go right then left with the track and continue with a hedge to your left. After about another 600m, the main track swings off to the right but we go forward to the field corner to pass through a hedge gap and continue with ditch to our left, to emerge onto a dirt lane (Moor Lane). Go right for about 150m and, immediately beyond kennels and farm building to your left, go left (leaving the Trent Valley Way) onto a finger-posted access drive. Pass beside a cottage to your left then through a gateway and continue, passing more farm buildings. Where the main track swings off to the left, go forward with a hedge to your right, to a stile in the corner of the garden. Cross and continue over the field beyond aiming for the left-hand end of a hedgeline which comes in from the right ahead. Arriving at the hedge end, continue forward again, now rising gently with a hedge to your right. At the top field corner, pass through a hedge gap then go immediately right with a hedge to your right. At the field corner, go left, still with the hedge right then follow the hedge as it swings to the right and continue onto a grassy lane and out onto a road in the village of South Scarle. Go forward through the village to the church.

It is an oddity of modern county boundaries that North Scarle should be in Lincolnshire while its neighbour, two miles to the south, is in Nottinghamshire. In Domesday Book we have just 'Scornelei', a word coming from the Old English meaning 'the mud or dung clearing'. The church of St Helen has a stumpy west tower with battlements and corner and intervening crocketed pinnacles, battlemented clerestory, aisles and south porch and a very plain chancel. There is a fine west window in the tower with what appears to be the outline of a much older opening above it. Above the south porch is an attractive little effigy of St Helen while, above the doorway itself, are some carved graffiti dating from 1704. Inside the building, there is a magnificent Norman north arcade while the south arcade, chancel and chancel arch come from the Early English period.

6. Return to the road and go left. Ignoring Church Lane to the right, continue down Main Street (signed as a cul-de-sac). Pass Wells Close and Washtub Lane to your left and follow the road as it bends to the left to leave the village. At a T-junction, go right along a surfaced lane. Ignore the access going off left to farm buildings and continue forward along what is now a dirt track. Just before the track bends into a field corner with, at the far side of the field a rail-crossing wicket gate, go right, as waymarked, over a plank bridge onto a headland path with a hedge/ditch to your left. 500m on, where the headland starts to bend to the right, go left through a finger-posted hedge gap and follow a ditch down to your left. We keep to the long curve of the ditch, which eventually takes us sharply to the left to join a farm track. Go right along the track with ditch and hedge to your left, soon crossing a major dike onto a road in the outskirts of Collingham. Go forward into the 30mph speed limit zone and between houses for 500m to the major junction with the A1133, with Low Street and The Grey Horse inn over. Cross to the pavement on the far side and go left, noting the stump of the old market cross at the junction with Queen Street and continue along High Street, passing Vicarage Close to your right. Take the next right onto Church Lane to find the entrance to the church grounds to your left.

All Saints has a noticeably low chancel, high clerestoried nave and low stumpy tower with battlements and relatively large corner crocketed pinnacles. Only the tower is so adorned, the remainder of the building exterior being very plain. The oldest part of the structure is to be found in the tower which although mainly Perpendicular and partially ruined by modern plaster rendering, has some Norman stonework in the west wall and Norman windows to the south. Most of what we see today dates from the 13th century including the arcades, font (although the wooden top is Jacobean), tower arch and chancel. The clerestory and north porch are Perpendicular (the south porch is a little more recent). The north door is believed to be the original oak one, carved on the outside but with the old planks clearly visible on the inside. The door has a much worn sanctuary ring to which those who claimed the right to sanctuary could cling. Inside the building, a list of incumbents traces Rectors as far back as Dominus Egidius de Erdyngton in 1262 and Hugh de Collingham (1286). There is a hatchment dating from 1808, a plaque to William Hart who died in 1703 and, in the floor at the east end of the north aisle, two worn effigies which are believed to date from the late 14th century. There are some interesting stones in the churchyard including one beneath a yew to the north-east commemorating two parishioners who served with the 17th Lancers and who fell at the Charge of the Light Brigade.

7. Leave the church by the path to the south-west which leads through a wicket gate onto Low Street. Bear left here, noting the markings on the wall showing water levels reached in 1795, 1875, 1947 and 1977. Opposite the water sub station over the road to your right, go left onto Temperance Lane and follow it as it twists its way to the A1133. Go right, passing Baptist Lane to your right and, just beyond the telephone box, cross the road to return to the car park and our start point.

22. Laxton – Egmanton – Moorhouse

Distance: 6½ miles (10.5km)

Maps: OS Landranger 120: Mansfield & Worksop, Sherwood Forest. OS Explorer 271: Newark-on-Trent; Retford, Southwell & Saxilby

Start: Laxton Visitor Centre (GR 724671) where there is ample parking, toilets and an adjacent inn.

Churches: St Michael, Laxton; The Parish and Shrine Church of Our Lady of Egmanton; Moorhouse church

The Walk

Our walk takes us from Laxton's magnificent church to its equally impressive castle remains then onwards along quiet lanes and field paths to the wonderful church at Egmanton. The fieldpath route to 'the church in the meadow' at Moorhouse might involve an encounter with livestock but an alternative along quiet country roads is also described. We return to our start point by quiet country lane, fieldpath and green lane.

Laxton is probably best known for its retention of the ancient strip farming system, for its Court Leet, its church and its castle. Today, as in medieval times, a large proportion of the village land is divided into three great open fields, the West (or Top), South (or Bottom) and Mill fields, and a number of enclosed areas. These in turn were divided into furlongs or strips, usually organised so that farmers had land of similar value. A feature of the system was that the houses and farm buildings tended to be located close to one another in the village and this is still the case in Laxton. Behind the farmhouses were (and are) closes which stretch away from the road towards back lanes and which in the past were used as orchards for growing crops or for keeping animals. The Court Leet still meets each year to administer the annual leases of the fields and also appoints a pinder to impound stray animals. The pinfold itself can be found close to the Dovecote Inn and is passed towards the end of Walk 23.

The Route

1. Before setting out on the walk, take time to browse the Visitor Centre which will put Laxton and its ancient field system into perspective. It is well worthwhile staying for the ten minutes it takes to watch the informative video and purchase of the guidebook is money well spent. Leave the car park and return to the road with the Dovecote Inn to your imme-

diate left. Cross, and bear right with the mini triangular green over to your right, then left, with the main road, to the church.

Saint Michael is a magnificent building for so small a village. The massive west tower is adorned with battlements and corner-crocketed pinnacles, gargoyles and a pyramid capping. There is a fine west door, tall south porch, south aisle and lovely clerestory, the latter being heavily pinnacled and decorated with crockets, gargoyles and frieze. The chancel is tall and relatively plain but is pierced with windows that make the interior of the church beautifully light and bright. Construction began in the 1190s but major changes to the structure were carried out between 1250 and 1260. The present chancel was built in the 14th century and Archbishop Rethread (Rotheram) of York had the clerestory built in the 15th century. Inside, he erected a rood screen, part of which survives in the chancel screen and also had his own effigy inserted against the north wall. Other monuments represent members of the de Everingham family and date between 1287 and 1398, that to Margery (who died in 1336) being the only Medieval oak effigy to be found in Nottingham. By the 19th century, the church was in disrepair and the building we see today is the result of a major restoration carried out around 1860 and financed by Earl Manvers, Lord of the Manor. The church was rededicated by the Bishop of Lincoln on 11th October, 1860 and a copy of the order of service can be found in the church. Also of interest is a list of vicars going back to Ric de Nottingham (1240) and Stephen de Lexington (1282) and of Lords of the Manor, starting with Geoffrey Alselin in 1086.

2. Return to Main Street and go straight over to enter a wide pathway where an explanation board tells us a little about the church. Continue forward along what soon becomes a green lane to arrive at a fieldgate. Our route goes right here, but an explanation board to the side should give encouragement to explore the site of Laxton's motte and bailey castle, which can be entered through a wicket gate ahead.

Laxton 'Castle' is probably the finest example of an 11th-century motte and bailey fortification to be found in Nottingham. The motte or mound occupies the highest point in the parish – 220ft above sea level and measures some 816ft in circumference and 71ft in height. The small mound on top, 8ft high, is unusual and may have been a lookout post. The motte would once have been topped by a wooden fortification and, again unusually, the fortification has two enclosures or baileys. Being close to Sherwood Forest, it would have acted as a venue for Forest Courts and would probably have received royal visitors from the times of Henry II to Edward I. The castle had fallen into disuse by the 14th century but during the first half of the 16th century the Roos family, lords of the manor, built a manor house here but by 1621 it was no longer in use and was demolished by the end of the 17th century. Today this is a lovely spot to roam and admire the impressive views to be had in all directions.

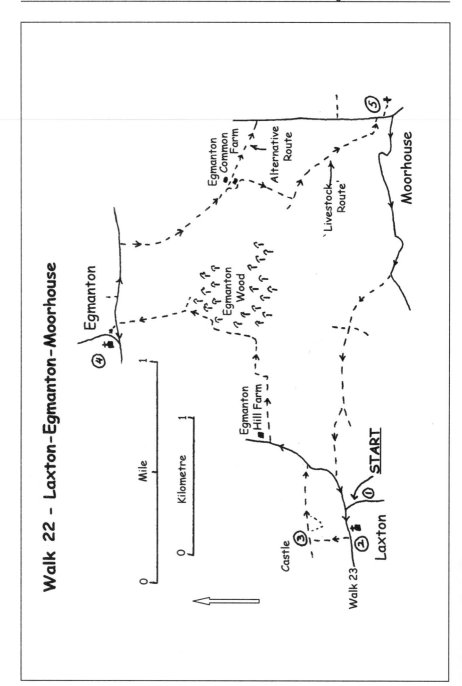

Walk 22 – Laxton–Egmanton–Moorhouse

3. If you have been to the castle site, pass back through the wicket gate and go left through a bridlegate and out into a field corner. Go forward with a hedge to your right and, 100m on, join a farm track. Go right, through another bridlegate beside fieldgate then left, along another track with a hedge over to your left. [Note that the definitive path continues towards the church that can be seen ahead, then veers back in a rather silly dog-leg. The landowner would prefer the route described be used rather than cause senseless damage to crops]. The track bears left through a hedge gap then right, onto a headland path with a hedge to the right and with views over to the left of all three Trent Valley power stations and, tucked away in the distance, the spire of Tuxford church. Pass through the gap at the field corner and continue forward along the headland to a finger-posted fieldgate that leads onto a minor road. Go left along the road and about 100m before the buildings of (Egmanton Hill) farm, go right through a wide finger-posted hedge gap onto a headland bridleway with a hedge to your left. At the field corner, pass through a hedge gap and go left, still with a hedge to your left. 150m on, go right onto what is usually a well-defined route between crops which rises gently to the trees of Egmanton Wood. At the wood edge, go left along a farm track with the trees to your right and soon, with views ahead over Egmanton village and Tuxford in the distance. Our path meanders gently downwards and at a T-junction, go left to dip, rise and dip again to the Weston Road in Egmanton. Go left along the road and at the T-junction (the Old Plough Inn is down to the left), go right to the church.

The attractive village of Egmanton is given as 'Agemuntone' in Domesday Book, which comes from the Old English meaning 'the farmstead of a man called Ecgmund'. Its most famous monument is its church and what a magnificent find this is! It is dedicated as The Parish and Shrine Church of Our Lady of Egmanton and is approached by a path which passes beside the base of an old market cross with the date 1692 inscribed at its base. It was a place of pilgrimage during the middle ages, following a vision by a local woman of the Virgin Mary. The practice died out, but was revived by the seventh Duke of Newcastle in 1896 and it was he who provided funds to restore the then-dilapidated building to its former glory. From the outside, this looks a very ordinary building with its 15th-century battlemented and pinnacled tower, nave, chancel, north aisle, clerestory and odd chapel-like structure to the south, which almost hides the southern entrance. Inside though, there are wonders to be found. The west doorway is a very ancient one, as is the plain font with its heavy metal top. Above and around the inside of the door is a wonderfully decorative and colourful organ cover, which is matched in colour and ornateness by the screen at the entrance to the chancel. In the chancel itself, the shrine image hangs on the wall and there are some wonderful tombstones in the floor and a fine hatchment. Set in the north wall is a memorial to William Cardinall dated 1598 and there is an interesting list of priests going back to Richard de Syreburn (Shireburn) in 1244. The most magnificent find of all though is the effigy in the side chapel with the epitaph – 'Good Christian folk who pass this way, for Baron Robert de Ayvill pray, at Egmanton he made his home, when Henry Beauclerc sat at the throne'. In the field behind the church itself is another fine example of a motte and bailey castle which measures some 20ft high and 460ft in circumference.

4. Return to the road and cross diagonally left to take a finger-posted footpath which cuts diagonally right over a field to the Weston road opposite Wood Lane – our approach route. Go left along the road and continue for 600m to the point where the road starts to rise. Here, go right onto a finger-posted farm track that meanders gently and soon rises to become a fine green lane. Approaching Egmanton Common Farm, pass through a metal half gate and continue to an area of hard-standing.

(At this point, you may either take the fieldpaths to Moorhouse where cattle may be encountered or the country lane route where no livestock will be met).

If the former, bear to the right here to pick up a finger-posted headland path with fence/hedges to your left and farm buildings over. At a double power post with junction box, go right, down the field, soon picking up a hedge to your left. At the bottom field corner, go left over a footbridge and stile and continue forward with ditch and hedge to your right. Pass beneath power cables and immediately beyond the next lone tree, go right over a stile and cross the field beyond, aiming for the huge power pylon in the distance, to arrive at the field corner. Cross the plank bridge and stile to the left then go right with a hedge to your right, passing the pylon we earlier used as our aiming point. Stay with the headland and pass through a stunted hedge gap and, at the next hedge/treeline, go left, keeping the bushes to your right. At the field corner, go right, through a gap then left, over a stile and onto a road in the village of Moorhouse. Go right, and 50m on, to the left, is the gateway into the meadow which contains the little chapel.

If you wish to avoid any chance of meeting livestock, continue forward, passing between the farm house and outbuildings and stay on the farm track to a minor country lane. Go right along the lane (take care, there are no verges but traffic is infrequent), to eventually enter the tiny village of Moorhouse, the fieldpath route coming in from the right opposite the village sign. 50m on, go left through a gateway into the meadow which contains the chapel.

The attractive little chapel at Moorhouse is set in the centre of a meadow heavily marked with ridge and furrow work which suggests earlier and extensive habitation. The building itself is a fairly plain rectangle built very much in the 12th-century French style with steeply slanting red-tiled roof and a double

The church at Moorhouse

bellcote set at a point which, internally would mark the division between nave and chancel. Outside, the only protrusions are a vestry to the north and a porch to the south-west, but the windows are a nice mixture of single lancets (sometimes grouped in pairs) and roundels. The church was built in 1860-61 with funds supplied by John Evelyn Denison, (Lord Ossington) whose tomb is to be found at Holy Rood church in Ossington.

5. Return to the road and go left. At the first junction, go right, signed to Laxton and Ollerton. Follow this meandering road for about three-quarters of a mile (take care, there are no verges), eventually walking a sharp bend to the right. At the next sharp bend (to the left), go right onto a farm track then almost immediately left onto a finger-posted headland path, quickly passing beneath power cables and continuing with ditch to your left. 400m on, go left, through a hedge gap and continue forward with hedge now to your right, eventually emerging onto a green lane. Continue forward on this earth and grass track that rises gently, then flattens, as Laxton church tower comes into view in the distance ahead. Stay with the main lane, ignoring all side paths, until arriving at a minor road. Go left and back to the village of Laxton to bear left at the little green, then left again at the Dovecote Inn and so back to our start point.

23. Laxton – Kneesall

Distance: 7¼ miles (11.5km)

Maps: OS Landranger 120: Mansfield & Worksop, Sherwood Forest. OS Explorer 28: Sherwood Forest (to be renumbered 270); 271: Newark-on-Trent; Retford, Southwell & Saxilby. Note: If you wish to use a 1:25,000 scale map, then you would be better off with the old, but still fairly accurate, Pathfinder 780 (Ollerton) since the entire walk is shown on a single side. Using the more modern Explorer maps will involve much folding and refolding since both sides will be required to cover the walk.

Start: Laxton Visitor Centre (GR 724671) where there is ample parking, toilets and an adjacent inn.

Churches: St Michael, Laxton; St Bartholomew, Kneesall

The Walk

Although again starting in Laxton, this is such an interesting area and such a good centre for walking that it would be a shame to miss the wonderful pathway system that stretches southwards to Kneesall with its fine church and taking in Laxton's Mill and West Fields. The walk itself is a very easy one on green lanes, headland paths, bridleways and country roads which can be undertaken at any time of the year — although parts of the route can become very muddy after wet weather and when horses have been on the tracks.

The Route

1. We begin in the same way as Walk 22 by returning to the road with the Dovecote Inn to our immediate left, crossing, and bearing right with the mini triangular green over to our right. Bear left with the main road signed to Boughton and Ollerton, which leads us to the church.

    Saint Michael has been described in some detail in the notes for Walk 22 but this magnificently proportioned structure is full of interest and well deserves a second visit. This time, perhaps a little more attention might be spent on the outside of the building where the walls of the tower and of the clerestory below the battlement stage are studded with fantastic gargoyles. On the north side can be found an effigy of Archbishop Rotherham who was Lord of the Manor in around 1480 and who was responsible for the wonderful clerestory and also for the internal screen. Note also the carved heads of King Edward I and his wife Eleanor to either side of the west door. They are said to have spent time in Laxton in 1290

– the Queen was to die at Harby in November of that year (see Walk 18). In the churchyard are the remains of the old Medieval cross. A millstone here is a reminder of the mills which were once so important to the village.

2. If you have visited the church, return to Main Street and go left (Walk 22 continued forward over the road) for about 300m, passing the Heritage Museum to your right. Where the road bends gently to the left signed to Boughton, go forward onto a lesser road signed as a cul-de-sac. Ignore the finger-posted footpath to the right and continue along the surfaced lane. Where the lane bends to the right as a stony track, go forward onto a

St Michael, Laxton

wide green way. (This point marks the junction of two important green lanes (also known as hollow ways since through heavy use, they quickly became deeply rutted). The track which we have just passed going off to the right leads to the eastern end of West Field, while the route we shall be following ahead leads to the southern section of the same field). Go forward along this fine sunken lane, ignoring the track going off to the left and continue gently up-slope between hedges. At the top of the slope, West Field (also known as Top Field) stretches off to our right. Continue along what has become a wide headland pathway with a hedge over to the left. At the field corner, where the main track bends to the right, cross a stile into the adjacent field corner and continue along the headland with a hedge to your left and with distant views, far over to the left, of Kneesall church tower. Follow the headland as it bends to the left, still with the hedge to your left. Where the hedge bends off to the left again, go right, across the field, aiming for a large lone tree that stands slightly to the right of farm buildings, to arrive on a minor road.

3. Go right along the road (the widest verges are on the far side), passing the Beth Shalom buildings to your left and, ignoring the finger-posted bridleway to the right, continue for a further 400m. Having passed an area of woodland in the field up to your right and coming opposite a finger-posted stony track off to the right which leads towards a large radio mast, go left onto a finger-posted bridleway with ditch to your right. Follow the main track forward into the trees and, at a waymarked cross-track go left to emerge from the wood. Bear left then right to pick up a headland path with a hedge to your right. This is a very long field but we eventually drop to the field corner to go left, still with the hedge to our right then, after about 80m, go right, through a wide hedge gap and forward up the field aiming for a lone tree on the skyline. Pass to the left of the tree and continue your line, passing another lone tree and going forward to the right-hand end of a hedgeline which comes in from the left. Go right here with ditch down to your left and with farm buildings to the front left. Follow the path as it bends to the left, now with a hedge to your right and opposite the far end of the farm buildings over to your right, go right, and keeping hedge to your right, arrive on a farm access track.

4. Go left along the track (Baulk Lane) which quickly improves to a surfaced lane and, after about three-quarters of a mile of good walking and wonderful views brings us to the village of Kneesall and a road crossing. Bear to the right (not sharply right), with the triangular green to your right. At the busy A616 go left, up-slope, passing the lovely brick hall over to your right, then the Village Hall to your left and so to the church.

Kneesall appears as 'Cheneshale' in Domesday Book but by 1175 it is given as 'Cneshala'. The probable meaning is 'the nook of land belonging to a man called Cyneheah' the latter being an Old English personal name. Today, it sits beside the busy A616 and is dominated by the church of St Bartholomew. This is a fine Nottinghamshire Perpendicular building with its west tower sporting a nicely decorated parapet and corner crocketed pinnacles, beneath which are placed grotesque corner gargoyles with more pleasant angels in between. The remainder of the building is plain although for some reason, the south side and east end of the large chancel have been decorated with battlements and crocketed pinnacles. The chancel, clerestory and aisle windows all date from the 15th century but the nave may be slightly earlier and the south doorway is probably late 13th century. On our way here, we passed the Old Hall, a rare early Tudor hunting lodge

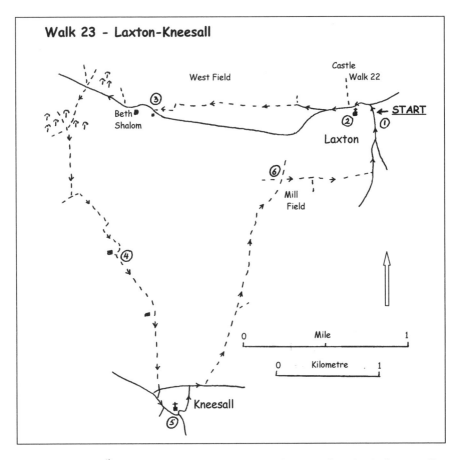

Walk 23 - Laxton-Kneesall

built in the 16th century by Sir John Hussey, Chief Butler of England. This is still a fine building but somehow, the modern glass in the windows looks a little out of place.

5. Return to the A616 and go left then left again (onto School Lane), passing the east end of the church up to your left. Follow the lane as it swings to the right then to the left, passing the school and arriving at a T-junction. Go right here for about 150m, then left onto a finger-posted earth and stone track, soon gaining views of Laxton church tower in the distance ahead. Our track deteriorates to a grassy way and ignoring the footpath off to the right we eventually drop down over a culvert/bridge and continue forward up a gentle incline through grassland. Stay with the main track, keeping a hedge over to the left as it meanders onwards and upwards. At the brow of the slope, continue forward along what is now

Mill Field, soon arriving at an information board and, just beyond it, a cross track. (Mill Field was first recorded in 1189 and has always been the largest of Laxton's open fields. In 1635 it comprised of 833 acres, 24 acres being strips of common grazing while most of the remainder was divided into 778 arable strips. Today, the field totals about 196 acres divided into 68 strips).

6. Go right at the cross-track and follow a path initially between fields, then continuing as a headland route with hedgeline to your right. On a clear day, Lincoln Cathedral can be made out far in the distance to your front left. Keep close up against the hedge as the path dips into a narrow sunken lane with hedges/trees to either side. Emerging through a fieldgate, continue forward along a wide track between trees/hedges to pass through fieldgates onto a minor road. Go left along the road and follow it as it bends to the right to re-enter Laxton village. At the junction, bear left, signed to Ollerton and Tuxford to pass the pinfold to your right just before the Dovecote Inn. Immediately beyond the Inn, go right to arrive back at our start point.

24. Haughton – Walesby – Bothamsall

Distance: 9½ miles (15km) (includes detour to St James, Haughton)

Maps: OS Landranger 120: Mansfield & Worksop, Sherwood Forest. OS Explorer 28: Sherwood Forest (to be renumbered 270)

Start: Haughton Corner Car Park (GR 681728). Ample space in the County Council car parking area east of the B6387.

Churches: St James, Haughton; St Edmund, Walesby; Our Lady and St Peter, Bothamsall

The Walk

Following sections of the Robin Hood Way, we wander over and around fields and through some lovely woodland on this walk. We cross and re-cross the rivers Meden and Maun, take in two fine churches, one of which we visited previously in Walk 15 and a short detour will give us sight of an interesting ruined chapel. Along the way, we shall bump into sections of path described in Walks 15 and 25 and these might be added as links should a longer excursion be contemplated.

We start our walk in the hamlet of Haughton which in Domesday Book appears as Hocton and comes from the Old English meaning 'the farmstead on a spur of land'. Today's Haughton comprises just a couple of houses and farms grouped close to the River Maun. Once though, Haughton was the home of the Stanhopes, becoming the seat of the Holles family, Earls of Clare in the 16th century. In 1770, Haughton was abandoned, the Earls of Clare having made their home at Welbeck. Nothing now remains of the old hall and even the church of St James is little more than a sad but romantic pile of rubble overgrown with trees and bushes.

The Route

1. Walk eastwards from the car parking area, away from the road, along a dirt and stone track. Go through a metal half-gate and stay with the track as it bends to pass beneath a railway bridge. At the point where the main track swings sharply to the right, leave it and go forward onto a headland path with the River Maun down to your left. [Note: the definitive pathline parallels our route, crossing the field about 100m to the right. However, walking the definitive line does little but cause damage to crops and thus the commonly walked and more pleasurable path is along the headland/river bank]. Pass through a hedge gap and over a

shallow ditch at the field corner and continue forward, still with the river down to your left. Soon the octagonal tower at Haughton Hall Farm comes into view to the left and, shortly beyond, we meet a major cross-track and join the Robin Hood Way.

2. Go right, away from the river, then follow the main track as it swings to the left. 150m on, at a junction, our route follows the main track to the right. [*] Follow the track now for a little over half a mile, passing through the edge of Lower Ponds Wood. The track eventually swings to the left and, 50m on from this point, go right over a waymarked stile (Robin Hood Way) into a field corner.

[*] If taking this walk in the winter when there are few leaves on the trees, it is well worth making a short detour to view, from a distance, the ruined chapel of St James. In this case, go straight on at the junction, keeping your eyes on a small copse over the field to the front left. 400m on, we are opposite the site but note that the field to the left and the ruins themselves are on private property. St James' became the domestic chapel of the Stanhope family in 1509. What is left comprises just sections of the nave walls with Norman stonework and a 14th-century arcade, which appears to have been blocked up when the aisle was removed. There are remnants of a Norman chancel arch and probably much more but now, all is rubble and overgrowth. Return to the junction and go left to rejoin the main route.

3. Continue forward along the headland with trees and beck to your left. At the field corner, go right with tree-line/bushes to your left and views of Walesby church far over to the left. (The line of the path from here to the outskirts of Walesby has recently changed and not all maps have been updated, so please follow these instructions). Continue the line with hedge initially to your left then to the right, eventually passing through a wide hedge gap at a field corner. Turn left along a farm track to arrive at cross-tracks close to a huge power pylon. The Robin Hood way goes to the right here but we go straight on, passing beneath the power cables with the pylon in the field to our right. Ours is now a fine green lane, which eventually improves to a surfaced road and leads us into Walesby where we meet Tuxford Road and the church opposite.

In Domesday Book, Walesby is given as 'Walesbi', meaning the 'farmstead/village of a man named Valr', the latter being an Old Scandinavian personal name. Our approach view of the church of St Edmund shows a striking north frontage of combined nave and clerestory adorned with battlements and pierced by magnificent windows. It is thought that the whole north wall was built in the 16th century using older materials. To the east is the chancel with its 14th-century windows and to the west, the fine 15th-century buttressed tower, battlemented,

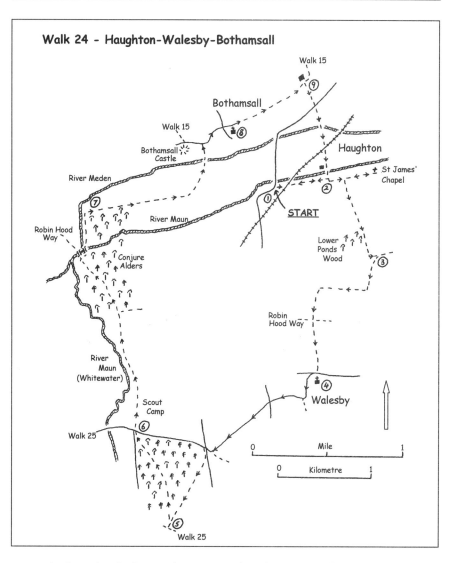

Walk 24 - Haughton-Walesby-Bothamsall

and adorned with the usual corner crocketed pinnacles. The south side of the church is a little less impressive although there is a nice south aisle, the arcades dating from the 13th century, and an unfortunately sealed porch.

4. Return to the road and go left then take the first left (Main Street), passing The Red Lion Inn over to your right. Follow Main Street as it swings to the right and continue to a major junction. Go diagonally left over the road to continue along Brake Road, signed to Thoresby and the Scout

Camp, with the Carpenter's Arms to your left. We pass a mobile home site then small trading estate to our right and stay with the road as it gently mounts towards woodland. Follow the road as it bends sharply to the right (ignoring the finger-posted bridleway to the left) and crosses a railway bridge then go immediately left onto a finger-posted path immediately before the woodland (Boughton Brake). Continue through bracken and gorse then bear right over low wooden barriers then left, along the path which leads into the trees. [Note: The definitive line of the bridleway follows the outside of Boughton Brake, keeping the woodland immediately to the right. However, there is full access to the Brake and a perfect path keeps parallel to the definitive but stays inside the trees – this is a much more pleasant route to walk]. Follow this lovely path with a thin screen of beeches to the left and thick (mainly coniferous) woodland to the right for about half a mile. Eventually, drop beneath overhead power cables with views of Boughton village through the trees ahead, to arrive on a major pressed-stone track.

5. Go sharply right up the stony path between the trees (we are walking in reverse a section of Walk 25 here) to pass through a wooden barrier and into an open glade with boulders strewn into rough circles. Continue through another barrier and go forward with the main path as it drops gently. At the first Y-junction, bear to the left and a few metres on, where the main path swings quite sharply to the left, go straight on into a magnificent beech wood to follow a wide earth and sand track. Ignore all side paths until emerging through wooden barriers and onto a road junction. (Walk 25 comes in from the left here)

6. Go straight over the junction to find a finger-posted bridleway beside a small parking area. Go forward on the main track (do not veer off to the left) which goes straight on between trees. [Note: There is a confusion of paths here but try to stay on the main route, which is well waymarked as a bridleway]. Soon we pass the Scout Camp to our right and before long the path runs along the top of sandstone cliffs with the River Maun (Whitewater) running along their base. Tucked into the cliff are a number of small rock shelters, one of which has been given the name Robin Hood's Cave. Stay with the main track as it passes over, then along the edge of heathland until crossing a stony track and entering thick woodland. Continue the line, ignoring all side tracks, the trees to the right slowly thinning out before resuming as thick woodland to either side. Stay with the main track as it swings right for a few metres then go left down a fairly steep slope to continue along a meandering path and join the confluence of the rivers Meden and Maun. This is a delightful

spot, originally known as Coningswath (King's Ford) which once stood on the King's Road from Blyth to Wellow and marked the eastern boundary of the hunting forest. Ignore the Robin Hood Way signs directing left over the first footbridge, and continue to the next footbridge. Go left here to cross the river and pick up a path with what is now the River Meden to your left and the area known as Conjure Alders to the right. (The name is a combination of Coningswath and Alder after the trees that grow here).

7. At the woodland corner, follow the track as it swings to the right, leaving the river behind but with trees still to your right. Continue along the track as it eventually leaves the trees behind and passes between open fields. To the front left now can be seen the tower of Bothamsall church and, on the skyline to the left, the mound of Bothamsall Castle. The track eventually bears to the left, crosses the River Meden and mounts gently to Main Street, Bothamsall. [This is the link with Walk 15]. Go right, through the village and to the church.

Bothamsall was originally an estate village of the Dukes of Newcastle. The name is certainly descriptive of its location since, in Domesday Book, it was spelt 'Bodmescel', coming from the Old English meaning 'the shelf by a broad river valley'. The church of Our Lady and St Peter, beautifully sited on a little mound,

Our Lady and St Peter, Bothamstall

was built in the Perpendicular style in 1845 to replace a 14th-century original. It is a compact mass of battlements, pinnacles and gargoyles with spindly tower complete with external stair turret and war memorial clock together with nicely proportioned nave, north aisle and chancel. Outside, nothing remains of the original building but internal stonework in the floor and the font apparently come from the 14th century.

8. Leave the church and descend to Main Street. Go *sharply* round to the right, (not Redhill Lane, signed to Crookford) onto Church Lane (signed as a cul-de-sac) with the church up to your right. Continue through a bridlegate beside fieldgate and on along what is now a grass and dirt lane. We go through two more field gates and pass the cupola-topped Haughton Park House Farm to our left to arrive on an access track with farm buildings to the front left. (Walk 15 approaches from the front here).

9. Go right along the access track (we are now back on the Robin Hood Way) and continue to the B6387. Cross the road with care and take the lane opposite signed to Haughton Hall Farm. We recross the River Meden then walk under a railway bridge, eventually skirting the buildings of Haughton Hall Farm with the strange octagonal tower to our right. Beyond the farm buildings, cross the bridge over the River Maun, pass through the bridlegate beside metal field gate then go immediately right, along the banks of the Maun (now down to the right), retracing our steps to the start point.

25. Wellow – Ollerton – Boughton

Distance: 9 miles (14.5km)

Maps: OS Landranger 120: Mansfield & Worksop, Sherwood Forest. OS Explorer 28: Sherwood Forest (to be renumbered 270)

Start: The village green at Wellow. There is limited parking at Wellow Memorial Hall on the west side of the green (GR 669661) but, if you use this facility, please 'park prettily'. If more than a couple of vehicles are involved, then there is ample parking at Wellow Dam north of the village (GR 668664). Directions from here to the church are described in Section 5 below. From the Memorial Hall, the church is reached by walking over the green and the Eakring road beyond to pass through the car park of the Olde Red Lion inn to the wicket gate, which gives access to the churchyard

Churches: St Swithin, Wellow; St Giles, Ollerton; St Matthew, Boughton

The Walk

A gentle stroll today, taking in three totally different style churches, some green and country lanes (plus very short sections of busy road) and meandering through patches of lovely woodland. In the middle of our ramble, we shall find ourselves repeating a short section of Walk 24.

Wellow presents itself very much as a traditional English village with its green, wonderful church, fine inns and a maypole. It does not appear in Domesday Book but in 1207 we have a 'Welhag' which comes from the Old English meaning 'the enclosure near a stream or spring'. The village was once protected by earthworks and the remains of the 13th-century Jordan Castle can still be found to the north-east. With the founding of Rufford Abbey in the 12th century, close links were maintained with its monks and these links continued with the Saviles and Dukes of Newcastle who owned Wellow following the Dissolution. The church of St Swithin is a beautiful red stone building with a very odd-looking external shape. The tower, sited at the south-west, is capped with Perpendicular battlements and corner crocketed pinnacles, each side spouting an off-centre gargoyle, but below this stage is 12th- and 13th-century work. Oddly, we have what appear to be two naves, side by side, but these are in fact a 14th-century nave with an exceptionally wide south aisle. The original building was constructed in the 12th century but was extended in the 13th and, of course, again during the Perpendicular period. Finally, there was a heavy restoration in 1878 when the chancel was entirely rebuilt.

The Route

1. Return to the Eakring road through the Olde Red Lion car park and go right to the busy A616 with the Durham Ox Inn opposite. Cross the road with care to go left, down slope and out of the village. Pass the entrance to Wellow Dam (our return route and alternative parking area) to the right and at the road junction beyond, go right, signed to Boughton and Retford. Pass beneath the railway bridge and, 200m on, go left into Wellow Green. A few metres down this short residential cul-de-sac, look out for a finger-posted gap to the right which takes us onto a path with wire

St Swithin, Wellow

fence and earth mound to our right and thick bushes/hedges to the left. 400m on, the path bends to the left to arrive at a track junction and three-way finger-post. Go right here, still with the fence and earth mound to your right and stay with the main path as it meanders gently to eventually pass beside a mobile home site (Fairholme Park) and arrive on a surfaced lane. Go forward then right over a railway bridge then bear left onto a stony lane which leads to the A616 and the outskirts of Ollerton. Go left along the road for a few metres then, crossing with the greatest of care, take the first right, signed to Ollerton Village. Ignore Bescar Lane to the left and continue with the main road as far as the White Hart Inn and the church opposite.

The old village of Ollerton is in complete contrast to its busy mining neighbour of New Ollerton. Here we have a pleasant village centre of babbling brook, church, old pubs and watermill, the latter dating from 1862 and being driven by the River

Walk 25 - Wellow-Ollerton-Boughton

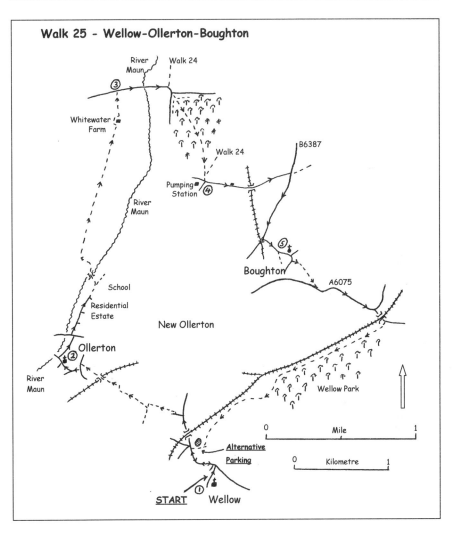

Maun which has supplied mills on this site since Norman times. In Domesday Book, the name is given as 'Alretun' which comes from the Old English meaning 'the farmstead where alder trees grow'. The importance of Ollerton came with the stagecoach for it was a major cross-roads for the routes from London to York, Newark to Worksop and Mansfield to Lincoln and the Hop Pole and White Hart became important coaching inns. The village was originally owned by the Nevilles and later by the Markhams who had held land in the area since 1260. In 1746, the Savile family, owners of Rufford, bought the estate but never really settled here. The church of St Giles is a very plain building, looking more pleasant from a distance than close to. What we see today is a relatively modern structure of 1780, which replaced an earlier ruin. The pleasing effect of stumpy tower capped with battlements and mini corner-crocketed pinnacles, long nave and short chancel is somewhat spoiled by the plain lancets which fill the nave walls. The whole, though, is nicely proportioned but perhaps the most interesting features are memories of the old church in the form of gravestones in the yard, some of them dating back to the 1670s and a memorial inside the church to Thomas Markham, an officer of Royalist Horse who was killed in a skirmish with Roundheads in 1643.

2. Drop down the steps onto the road to go right then right again, keeping the churchyard wall to your right. Continue with The Hop Pole inn (a reminder that there were once hop yards and markets here) to your right then The Snooty Fox to the left and continue to the junction with the A616. Go left, but cross the road with the greatest of care and as quickly as possible. Then, go right immediately beyond the electricity sub-station box and before crossing the river, where a finger-post takes us down onto the end of a cul-de-sac (Maida Lane). Continue forward through the housing estate, passing Glasby Court then De Lacy Court where the road deteriorates to a stony track. Passing Dove Croft to your right and eventually leaving the houses behind, go left onto a finger-posted path (the main route continues ahead here). Stay with the path for about a mile and a half as it bends to cross a bridleway bridge over the River Maun then swings northwards on a straight line, skirting around the edge of Whitewater Farm to eventually emerge onto Whitewater Lane.

3. Go right along the lane (taking care since verges are minimal or non-existent), crossing the little hump backed bridge over the Maun and continuing to the road junction which we passed in Walk 24. At the point where the main road bends left to Walesby and another goes right to Ollerton, go straight on, leaving the road and crossing onto the grass and passing through a low wood barrier. At the junction of tracks at the wood edge, take the centre path, which drives forward into beautiful broadleaf woodland (we are walking a section of Walk 24 in reverse here). Stay with the main path that continues in a more or less straight line, eventually joining a stony track which comes in from the right. Go forward again on this and continue through a low wooden barrier into a grassy glade with stones strewn into a rough circle. Pass through another barrier and drop gently to eventually leave the trees and join a surfaced lane with Boughton Pumping Station behind the trees to the front right (Walk 24 came in from the left just before this point).

4. Go left along the lane and continue all the way to the busy B6387. Cross with care to the walkway in the far verge and ignoring the finger-posted path opposite, go right into Boughton. Entering the built up part of the village, go left onto Church Road just as the main road bends right to pass beneath the railway and continue to the little triangular green with the church to the left.

This part of Boughton is an attractive little village in its own right, hidden from its busy neighbour of New Ollerton. In Domesday Book, we have 'Buchetone', which comes from the Old English and probably means 'the farmstead of a man named Bucca' although an alternative meaning could be 'the farmstead where bucks (or he goats) are kept'. The church of St Matthew is a relatively modern building, having been constructed by James Fowler of Louth, Lincolnshire, in 1867 however, older gravestones to be found in the churchyard indicate an earlier structure. The church itself comprises a plain nave and chancel with tower, capped with a nice little broach spire. The porch hugs the side of the tower and there is a fine east window, which commemorates WJ Pickin, who died in 1869 and was an agent to the Duke of Newcastle. It is a very plain building but sits beautifully here beside the old school and the tiny village green.

5. Return to the road and bear round to the left over the junction (not sharply left into Church Lane). Keeping the green to your left, follow the main road round to the right for about 100m then go left down a finger-posted lane which ends in a mini-residential cul-de-sac. At the road end, cross the stile into field edge and bear slightly right, passing immediately to the left of a double power post. Continue over the field to arrive at a shallow embankment up onto the A6075, with industrial estate buildings over. Go left along the pavement of this busy road, which passes through the Boughton industrial estates. About 700m on, where the road bends sharply left, signed to Kirton and Tuxford, cross with the greatest of care to go forward on a lesser road signed to Laxton. Pass beneath the railway arch, then go immediately right onto a finger-posted track. At the Y-junction, take the waymarked left branch into the woodland and pass through a wooden barrier to enter Wellow Park. Stay with the main track which meanders with a thin screen of trees to your right and thick woodland to the left for almost a mile, (a very muddy mile after wet weather) eventually emerging onto a green and grassy lane. Stay with the main route which meanders onwards to eventually pass the cricket pitch to your left then bear right with Wellow dam to the right (alternative parking to the left here) and so onto the A616. Go left, gently rising into the village and with the Durham Ox Inn to your left, go right onto Eakring Road and so back to the green and the start point.

26. Rufford Abbey – Edwinstowe – Major Oak – Centre Tree

Distance: 9 miles (14.5km)

Maps: OS Landranger 120: Mansfield & Worksop, Sherwood Forest. OS Explorer 28: Sherwood Forest (to be renumbered 270)

Start: Rufford Abbey (GR 643647). Ample parking at the Abbey Car Park where a small charge is made during the tourist season.

Churches: Rufford Abbey; St Mary, Edwinstowe

The Walk

Starting at Rufford Abbey, we skirt its lake then follow headland paths to Edwinstowe which, according to legend, has close links with Robin Hood and Maid Marian. Here we pick up the Robin Hood Way and continue through Sherwood Forest, calling in at the Visitor Centre and visiting Major

Rufford Abbey

Oak and Centre Tree. Finally, after crossing the River Maun, we return by mainly field edge paths to our start point.

Rufford Abbey is now little more than a romantic ruin standing in some 130 acres of lovely parkland managed by English Heritage. The Abbey was founded as a Cistercian house in 1146 although major building work continued until the 1170s. The monks here were not always a well-behaved lot and there were constant clashes with the authorities during the 13th century over their infringements of the strict forest laws. In 1280, one of their members was arrested for murdering a fellow monk and in 1307, two members of the house were accused of highway robbery! In a survey of 1535, the abbey's annual income was only £176 (compared with £1115 at Fountains) and the following year, the house was dissolved. In 1537, the property was granted to George Talbot, 4th Earl of Shrewsbury but it was not until the 6th Earl, who was the fourth husband of Bess of Hardwick, that any work was done on the site. He transformed the old Abbey into a private country house, expansion continuing under Gilbert Talbot, the 7th Earl. The family died out in 1626 and the estate passed to Sir George Savile. The family remained Royalist during the Civil War and following the Restoration they were granted the title of Viscounts then Earls and finally, in 1685, Marquess of Halifax. Rufford now became a magnificent house, the old monastery being pulled down and a wonderful country mansion replacing it. Subsequent owners carried out major works on the gardens but at the end of the day, taxation forced the sale of the site in 1938. It was finally acquired by Nottinghamshire County Council in 1956 who dismantled most of what was by then a dangerous relic. Fortunately, with the help of English Heritage, some restoration has been achieved and we have the picturesque ruin of today.

The Route

1. From the car park, walk across to the old Abbey building and mount the steps into what would have been the lay dormitory. Go left, through the room, noting especially the fine gargoyles on the walls and descend 'the night stairs' which would have given easy access to services held in the Abbey church beyond (the outline of the church building is marked with stones in the lawn). If you follow the walls around to the right now, you will find an entrance onto the cellars where there is usually an exhibition giving a history of the Abbey. To continue our walk, from the bottom of 'the night stairs', aim diagonally right over the lawns, passing to the left of a huge stone urn standing on the grass to arrive at a junction of gravel tracks. Bear left here, keeping a wooden fence to your right and following the signs for 'Mill via Lakeside Walk'. Continue along the main path and, at the next junction, go right, crossing a footbridge and contin-

uing along a pleasant pathway which skirts the lake which is to the left. Stay with this path all the way to the north-east corner of the lake, where a bridge goes off to the left and continues over a dam to the old mill building. *Do not cross this bridge, but go straight on* along a path that drops down to pass through a gateway onto a country lane. Go straight over and walk a finger-posted headland route with hedgeline to your left. Stay on this line, eventually losing the hedge to the left and picking up a stunted version to the right. Pass an area of woodland up an embankment to your right and continue forward to meet the busy A614 with the railway bridge to your right.

2. Cross the road with care to a stile on the far side and follow a narrow pathway with bushes to the left and railway embankment up to the right. Cross a footbridge over a drain then continue for a few metres to cross a stile to the left and go immediately right to continue the line along a headland path/track with railway embankment up to your right. We stay on this line for about a mile and a half, the path gently rising at first with the railway dipping into a cutting. Dropping down the far incline, we get good views of Edwinstowe and its church to the front right. Pass the Thoresby Colliery Signal Box and eventually pick up garden fences and hedges to the left and arrive on a main road. Go right, passing beneath the railway bridge and into the outskirts of Edwinstowe. The Dukeries inn with its carvings of Robin Hood and his merry men to our right was built in 1890 to cater for the railway tourists; it was famous for its huge ballroom, which was unfortunately destroyed by a fire in 1929. Just beyond, we pass Boy Lane to the right and, opposite, appropriately enough, Friend Lane. Continue along the main road (High Street), crossing the River Maun with its little conservation area and passing the Black Swan then Ye Olde Jug & Glass (over the road to the left is a fine sculpture of Robin Hood and Maid Marian), to arrive at cross-roads with the Royal Oak inn on the corner to the right. Cross the junction with care and continue up Church Street opposite, passing The Forest Lodge Hotel then, taking care again, cross to the *second* gateway into the grounds of the church. (Before entering the church grounds, note the plaque on the outside wall, which informs us that this is the end-point of the 105 mile-long Robin Hood Way path).

Edwinstowe is spelt 'Edenestou' in Domesday Book and takes its name from 'the resting place' or 'holy shrine' of King Edwin'. Edwin was the Christian Saxon king of Northumbria who came south from York in 633 to do battle with King Penda of Mercia and was killed in the subsequent Battle of Heathfield/Hatfield – adjacent to nearby Cuckney. (Some believe that the Hatfield referred to is the one near Doncaster). Following the Norman Conquest, the town was brought within the

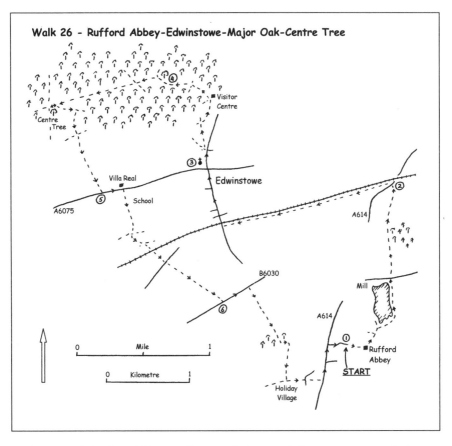

Walk 26 - Rufford Abbey-Edwinstowe-Major Oak-Centre Tree

bounds of The Royal Hunting Forest of Sherwood. The area remained almost entirely dependent on agriculture and crafts associated with the forest until the arrival of the railway in Worksop in 1849, which brought the first 'Dukeries tourists' to Edwinstowe. The greatest change though took place in 1925 when the first shaft at Thoresby Colliery was sunk. This attracted large numbers of miners and their families from all over Britain and brought significant alterations to the town. Today, it is still a great visitor attraction with its fine church, excellent hostelries and the wonderful forest nearby. A notice outside the lovely church of St Mary tells us that this is the place where Robin Hood and Maid Marian are said to have been married. Notwithstanding the legend, it is believed that a place of worship was first set up here in 633 AD to mark the spot where King Edwin was finally buried following his death at the Battle of Hatfield. Today's building though is a much later structure, its establishment having been ordered by Henry II in 1175 as part of his penance for involvement in the murder of Thomas à Becket –

their heads can be seen staring at each other across the nave! Now, we have a much-battlemented building, which includes a west tower surmounted by a beautiful broach spire with ornamental turrets. The tower probably dates from the 12th century and has a most unusually tall west lancet divided by a transom. The original spire was erected around 1400 (the turrets were probably added two hundred years later), but was struck by lightning and collapsed in 1672 and today's structure is a 19th-century replica. There is a small Norman doorway in the south wall of the chancel but much of what can be seen today dates from the 14th century. The east window is of the Decorated period, while the clerestory and battlemented finishes to the building are Perpendicular. Inside the church, there are memorials to the Rigley-Wards and to William Villa Real, a member of a Portuguese-Jewish family who settled in the area in the 18th century. Affixed to the north interior wall is 'the Forest Measure' which is believed to have been an ancient rule for measuring land (or perhaps timber), and a bronze crucifix which was found near Givenchy in France during the First World War and was brought back and mounted here. In the churchyard, at the top of the steps leading from the south gateway, there is an interesting gravestone to Henry James Perrener, an Officer of the Bow Street Runners who died in 1841.

3. Return to Church Street and go left, soon passing the Edwinstowe village sign. Shortly beyond, at the end-of-speed-restriction sign, cross Forest Corner (lane) and take the finger-posted footpath (Robin Hood Way) which starts between the huge Sherwood Forest Country Park board and the Edwinstowe Village Trail notice board and which leads between the cricket pitch to the left and the road to your right. Continue along the track, signed to Visitor Centre and Major Oak Tree and, at the top of the slope at cross-tracks, go right, with the Robin Hood Way sign, still signed to Visitor Centre and Major Oak. Pass a play area to your right and stay with the main path as it skirts car parks, crosses access roads and, following the signed pathway, eventually leads to the Visitor Centre entrance. (This is well worth a visit. There are toilets here as well as a permanent exhibition about the forest, Information Centre and gift shops). Our route though goes left immediately before the entrance and at the Y-junction a few metres on, we go forward (the BLUE trail, signed to Major Oak) with the Visitor Centre over the fence to the right. Follow the main path, which meanders through this wonderful oak woodland, eventually arriving at the Major Oak glade.

What a sad sight this tree is today, supported as it is with great baulks of timber. It is still imposing, being some 65ft in height, 33ft in circumference and perhaps six or seven hundred years old. It has been a great attraction since Victorian times when the railway started bringing tourists to the area and of course, it is here that legend has it that Robin Hood and his men met together.

Its earliest recorded name is the Cock Pen Tree, for, in the 18th century, its hollow centre was used as a pen for cockerels before they were released and used for the sport of cock fighting. In 1790, a Major Hayman Rooke, a local historian, described the tree in his book on Sherwood oaks and shortly afterwards, the tree was called after him, the name meaning literally 'The Major's Oak'. Amongst the many famous visits to Major Oak was that of over 30 suffragettes, including Mrs Emiline Pankhurst in 1912. All thirty are said to have stood inside the oak, thus setting a new record for the time!

4. Continue along the main path, keeping the wooden fence with Major Oak behind to your right. Follow the path as it bears to the right signed to Visitor Centre and where the path swings to the right again, go left on a narrower trail (signed as Robin Hood Way with a partially hidden waymarker low down to the right). The path improves to what was once a tarmac track but which is now much deteriorated. Ignore all side paths and stay with what is now The Robin Hood Way (also waymarked as the RED forest trail) for about three-quarters of a mile, eventually arriving at a metal half-gate over the track. Just beyond and to the left is the Centre Tree. (The Robin Hood Way goes forward then to the right here). (It is doubtful that this particular tree marked the centre of Sherwood Forest. What is certain is that in 1709, the Duke of Newcastle cut two broad avenues running east-west and north-south, 20m and 30m wide, through the heart of the forest and that the tree marked the junction of those drives. In 1842, the Duke of Portland built Archway Lodge at the southern start of the avenue. It was intended to be a gatehouse on a magnificent green ride from Welbeck Abbey to Nottingham but the link was never completed). Retrace your steps back along the path, passing through the metal half-gate and, 60m on, bear right, passing through another metal half-gate and picking up a grassy path through the trees. 300m on, at cross-tracks, go right, dropping gently for about 100m and at an indistinct Y-junction, bear left on an earthy path which continues down an incline to cross a bridleway and out of the woodland. Continue forward along what is now a headland path with hedgeline initially to your left but which slowly improves to a laneway and leads to the A6075 (Mansfield Road).

5. Go left along the pavement to enter the outskirts of Edwinstowe. Pass into the 30mph speed limit zone and, coming abreast of the main cottage of Villa Real Farm to your left, cross the road with care to go right down a finger-posted lane with school and playing fields over hedge to the left. At the bottom of the incline, follow the main path round to the right for about 25m, then leave the track to go left. Ignore the finger-posted path to the left and go forward between fields to a bridleway bridge over the

River Maun. Cross, and follow the path as it swings to the left, the river down to your left now and hedge to the right. Where the hedge ends, go right on an upward sloping headland path with a hedge to your right. Cross the railway line with care then continue forward, still gently up-slope, on the headland path. At a lane, go straight over and continue the line that dips and climbs with a hedge to your right to eventually pass beside a cottage and arrive on the B6030.

6. Go left along the pavement for about 400m and, at the point where there is a traffic island in the middle of the road and before the leisure complex, cross the road to pick up a track which drops away at a right-angle from the road. Our route, still the Robin Hood Way, becomes a headland path with the hedge to the left as it drops then rises to a patch of woodland. Pass through the trees and at the far side, go left with the woodland to your left then, at the field corner, go right on a headland path which drops gently with a hedge to the left. At the bottom of the slope we arrive on a stony lane where we go left to join the Holiday Village road, which comes in from the right. Go straight on along the road and where this bends to the left, *go straight on* again along a finger-posted dirt and stone track (sometimes gated) which leads to the busy A614. Cross the road with care and go left, up-slope. At the top, take the second road to the right and so back into Rufford Abbey Car Park.

27. Carburton – Hardwick – Clumber

Distance: 9½ miles (15km)

Maps: OS Landranger 120: Mansfield & Worksop, Sherwood Forest. OS Explorer 28: Sherwood Forest (to be renumbered 270)

Start: Large car parking area 700m north-east of Truman's Lodge (GR 611761)

Churches: St Giles, Carburton; Clumber Chapel

The Walk

Clumber Park is a magnificent walking area and today's wander follows good paths through forest and along the edge of the lake. It takes in a short section of country road and links the beautifully ugly little church of Carburton with the splendour of the estate chapel at Clumber itself, skirting the hamlet of Hardwick on the way. This is one of the longer walks in the book but it may be shortened to about 5½ miles (9kms) should you wish for a less demanding stroll.

Our walk begins at the northern edge of Clumber Park, a truly wonderful recreation facility covering some 4,000 acres of forest, lake, heath and grassland which can be easily accessed by excellent footpaths and cycle tracks – all managed by the National Trust. Originally part of Sherwood Forest, a license was granted to the Duke of Newcastle in 1707 to enclose it as a hunting park for Queen Anne. In 1767, the 2nd Duke decided to move the family seat from Haughton and work began on a mansion to match Chatsworth beside what is now the lake. The designer, Stephen Wright also undertook the layout of a number of lodges and gateways through which the Park could be entered. The River Poulter, which ran in front of the house, was dammed. A magnificent lake was created with a fine bridge crossing it to the south-west and, by the 19th-century, Clumber had become the country seat of the Dukes of Newcastle. The house was burnt down in 1879 but was rebuilt and filled with a magnificent collection of paintings and rare books. The dukes of this period were a hard lot and the 4th Duke for instance, who was opposed to parliamentary reform, evicted some of his tenants when they refused to vote for his parliamentary candidate. When the same thing happened in 1831, he threatened to double their rents. As a result, his mansion, Nottingham Castle, was burnt by a mob. He died in 1851 and was buried with his Duchess at the mausoleum in Milton. His successor, the 5th Duke was an influential government figure, holding the position of Secretary of State for War at the time of the Crimean conflict and it was he who planted Clumber's famous Lime Tree Avenue. The 6th Duke inherited the estate in 1864 and built a new chapel. However, shortly after his death in 1879, fire severely damaged part of the house and it was the 7th Duke who rebuilt it and started work on the beautiful church that we see today. Unfortunately, following his death in 1928, the Park went into decline. The estate passed to his nephew, the Earl of Lincoln, but high taxation resulted in the treasures being dispersed and sold. The house was demolished in 1938, only the stable block and the Duke's study (now housing the National Trust shop, restaurant and information centre) remaining to indicate what a magnificent complex this must have been. During the Second World War, the park was used by the War Office for the storage of ammunition, training and the trial of new military hardware. Following the War the area was acquired by the National Trust who have managed it so well ever since.

The Route

1. Return to the road and go right for about 700m to a T-junction then left through the gateway of Truman's Lodge. This is one of five structures which guard the entrance to Clumber and which were designed by Stephen Wright. It is named after John Truman who once lived here. [Note: the road section to the lodge can be avoided by taking an 'unofficial' alternative along the well-walked path which starts from the north-west corner of the car park and runs north of and parallel to the road but rejoins it just short of the T-junction]. 150m on, opposite the sign giving details of park entry charges (for vehicles), go right through a wooden barrier and onto a forestry track through the trees. We *stay with the main track* which is surfaced or stony throughout though in many places potholed and worn. This is a wonderful undulating and gently meandering woodland route, which drives its way in a generally south-easterly direction for almost a mile and three quarters to eventually pass through more wooden barriers and arrive on another of the estate's surfaced lanes. Go right, down the lane, crossing the River Poulter bridge, passing through Carburton Gate, (another of Wright's designs), then a secondary lodge to enter the 'village' of Carburton with sight of the church over to the front right. Pass a red brick cottage to your right then where the road bends gently to the left with stables entrance and post box left, go right up a lane signed as a cul-de-sac which leads to the church.

    The tiny village of Carburton consists of little more than a couple of farms and a church. In Domesday Book, it is spelt 'Carbertone' which is of Old English derivation and could possibly translate as 'the barley farm/outlying grange where

Walk 27 - Carburton-Hardwick-Clumber

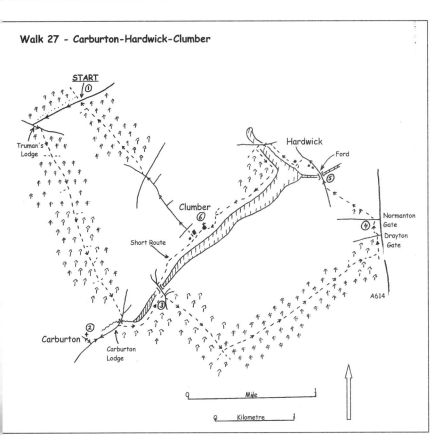

corn is stored'. In the 11th century, Carburton formed part of the Royal Hunting Manor of Mansfield and was probably a much larger place than it is today. Later, sometime between 1615 and 1707, the village was reduced in size from about 21 to just three or four houses, which is about what we have today! The church of St Giles looks a total mess from the outside, in fact, from a distance it resembles an old air raid shelter. The problem is that it has been over-restored and finished with a rendering of plaster and concrete, this done around 1958. This desecration has left us with an ungainly combined nave and chancel with ugly south porch and even uglier bellcote. The east end of the building seems to have been stuck on to keep the rain out! However, a little examination reveals this as a wonderful Norman building, the three arcades in the south wall into which silly off-centre windows have been placed, showing that there was once a south aisle. Inside the building, there are beautiful but simple 13th-century windows and a very plain Norman tub font. The actual foundation of the church is obscure but it is built on a 12th-century Anglo-Norman plan and a photograph of 1790 reveals a slightly different structure from the one we see here. The 'memorial' history of the church is a little difficult to find but behind the altar there are some fine stones set into the floor which date from the 18ᵗʰ century. Even more interesting is a brass plate to John Mazine. He was equerry to the 1ˢᵗ Duke of Newcastle at the battle of Marston Moor in 1644 when the Royalists under Prince Rupert suffered defeat and the Duke sought refuge abroad. Mazine was appointed Master of Horse by the Duke at his riding school in Antwerp and on his return to England, continued the appointment in the riding school which the Duke created at Welbeck.

2. Retrace your steps to pass back through Carburton Gate and, 50m on, opposite the National Trust board giving vehicle entry prices to the park, go right onto a narrow footpath which leads into the trees. We soon pick up the south-east end of Clumber Lake and follow this beautiful feature, which is down to our left as the path meanders through the edge of wonderful woodland. There are several side tracks as we progress but stay on the main well-walked path closest to the lake edge (usually seen through a screen of trees and bushes to the left) all the way to a junction of surfaced lanes with the lovely Clumber Bridge to the left.

    Here the route may be shortened by some four miles by walking directly to Clumber Chapel where the main walk is rejoined. To achieve this:

3a. Go left over the bridge where there are magnificent views of Clumber Chapel with the lake in the foreground up to the right. On the far side, just before the junction of estate roads, go right onto a minor but well-walked footpath, which drops down amongst trees with the lake visible through a screen of bushes to your right. Soon we pick up a paling fence to the right, which we follow as it skirts the edge of the old Clumber Grotto with a red brick building to the left. Continue along the main path, keeping the lake down to your right, eventually leaving the woodland to be suddenly faced with the majesty of Clumber Chapel ahead. Stay with the path closest to the lakeside until being forced to the left and onto a gravelled driveway. Go right, up a couple of steps and onto the lawn of the old house and the chapel grounds with the stable block up to the front left and the chapel a little beyond. Wander up towards the chapel.

    Clumber Chapel was built as a private place of worship for the estate and was originally dedicated to The Blessed Trinity by the Bishop of Southwell in 1889. Its dedication was later changed to St Mary the Virgin. It was the third of the chapels to be built for the Dukes at Clumber and cost £30,000. The architect was G.F. Bodley. This is a magnificent cruciform building in the Gothic Revival style. It is of white Steetly stone and red Runcorn sandstone which are banded together to make a fitting addition to the beauty of its surroundings. There is a lofty nave and chancel of equal height with shorter transepts, which form the crossing. Above the centre-point rises a pinnacled tower, surmounted by an octagonal corona supported by flying buttresses and above, a magnificent spire reaching to a height of 180ft. Inside, the building is a dream of airy unclutteredness. At the east end is a fine oak screen with rood above and beyond is the magnificent east window.

At this point the two walks join again. See paragraph 6 for the continuation.

Clumber Chapel

3. To continue the longer walk, do not cross the bridge but go sharply to the right, signed to South Lodge (No Through Road), for a few metres then left through a wooden barrier and onto a woodland track. Stay with the main pathway as it rises gently, ignoring all side tracks to arrive, after about ten minutes, at another wooden barrier and T-junction (a minor path continues ahead). Go left along the wide pathway with yew trees initially to your left as it undulates gently through more magnificent woodland. (At the time of writing, this was marked as the Red cycle trail, so, if these signs are still in use, follow them). Stay with the main track, which eventually becomes stony and where it swings to the left, go forward along a narrower path between broadleaf trees (still marked as the Red cycle trail). Our path eventually bears to the right, passing an old wooden barrier and now, to the front behind the tree-line we can hear, then see, vehicles rushing along the A614. At a major T-junction of tracks with the National Trust sign to your right, go left along a meandering path to arrive on a surfaced estate lane with Drayton Gate to the left. This is another Wright structure and was one of the main gateways to the estate, which, with Drayton Avenue on the far side of the road, marked the start of the drive to the mausoleum at Milton. Go straight over the lane and bear to the left on the Red cycle trail (also marked as the Robin Hood Way). Our path skirts the edge of the gateway which can be seen through the trees to the left, then swings to the right to follow the edge of thick woodland to the right, eventually arriving on another estate lane with Normanton Gate up to the right. This is the odd one out of the Clumber gates in that it is not a Wright structure. It dates from around 1700 and comes from Shireoaks, where it once gave access to the Hall there.

4. Cross the lane and pass through a finger-posted bridlegate (signed as the Robin Hood Way). Follow the angle of the finger-post, cutting off the corner of the field and aiming for the right-hand external corner of fenced woodland ahead. The path follows the woodland fence for a short distance, then drops in the direction of the left-hand edge of cottages of Hardwick in the valley below. We emerge through a gap at the bottom field corner and onto an estate road. Go right, along the road, crossing the ford by the footbridge, to enter the outskirts of Hardwick, built by the 7th Duke of Newcastle for his workers in the late 19th century.

5. Pass the stable and barns to your left and where the road swings to the right, go left with the Robin Hood Way waymarker, also signed to car park and toilets (the Red cycle route continues along the road here). Cross the car-parking area and continue down the narrow alley with the toilet block to your right to arrive on the lake shore. Go right along the path, keeping the lake to your left, soon passing through another parking area to arrive on a surfaced lane. Go left along the lane with the main lake to your left and an extension to the right. Half way over this causeway, go left, with the Green Cycle Trail marker (also the Robin Hood Way), passing between wooden fences with lakes to either side. At the end of the lakes and at a junction, go left, leaving the Cycle Trail which continues onwards, with the main Clumber Lake through bushes and trees to the left. We keep the lake to our left now, often behind a thin screen of trees and bushes. [Note: there are many paths along the lake edge and at varying distances from it but provided the lake is to your left, any path you take will eventually lead to the chapel, our next port of call]. Whichever path is taken, we shall eventually be forced away from the immediate lakeside and find ourselves separated from it by a field. Soon, all paths lead to a cross-track where we go left to pass through a narrow stone gateway (the cycle track goes off to the right) and into rhododendron bushes

and yew trees at the edge of the chapel grounds. Stay with the main path, which bears to the left to arrive on the fine promenade at the lake edge again. To the left is the old boat dock. (From here, two miniature sailing boats, the Lincoln and the Salamanca, once glided over the lake. The Lincoln was originally used as a floating summerhouse but more recently, the resident vicar used them for fishing trips on the lake. The ribs of one of them can sometimes be seen offshore from the dock, the boat having been sunk when children were able to board it when the lake was frozen and started a fire on it). Our way onwards goes right along the gravel promenade with the lake to the left. (Here the path is decorated with short sections of steps and ornamental marble and stone benches. On the far side of the lake can be seen a little summer house built in the form of a Greek temple with Doric columns, another Wright monument). Continue between more rhododendrons and soon the magnificent church of St Mary the Virgin in its wonderful setting appears up to the right.

6. Leaving the chapel (usually by the west door), follow the gravel path which skirts the edge of the stable block (to your right). Go right into the yard with the clock tower, café and shop to your right and toilets to the left. At the fork in the yard, take the left-hand path through a gateway and out onto a crossing of estate roads with large car park up to your right. Go straight on along the road, gently up the incline and passing the cricket pitch with its lovely pavilion over to your right. Pass a lane to the right signed to the Conservation Centre and another signed to Hardwick Village to arrive at crossroads. Up to the right here is Clumber's famous lime tree avenue but we go straight over, signed for Truman's Lodge. A little under 100m on, leave the road to bear right onto a stony path (usually finger-posted as Robin Hood Way) into magnificent broadleaf woodland. Stay with the main path as it drives in a more-or-less straight line for almost three-quarters of a mile, ignoring the cycle track that eventually swings off to the left. Eventually, arrive at a road with, on the far side, our start point.

28. Cuckney – Church Warsop – Hazel Gap – Norton

Distance: 8½ miles (13.5km)

Maps: OS Landranger 120: Mansfield & Worksop, Sherwood Forest. OS Explorer 28: Sherwood Forest (to be renumbered 270)

Start: The Village Hall, immediately to the south of the church at Cuckney (GR 566713). Although there is ample space here, if more than a few cars are to use the facility, please check with the keyholder or use alternative parking at the picnic site beside the River Meden, south of the church in Church Warsop (GR 568686) and start the walk from paragraph 3 [*] below.

Churches: St Mary, Cuckney; St Peter and St Paul, Warsop

The Walk

A lovely walk, much of it along sections of the Robin Hood Way, over fields, along country lanes and green lanes and through some magnificent forest, taking in two beautiful churches and passing over the site of an ancient castle.

We start our walk in the attractive little village of Cuckney, one of the estate villages of the Dukes of Portland whose seat is at Welbeck Abbey (see Walk 30). It is one of those 'perfect' villages with some fine houses, a great pub, a wonderful church and the earthwork mounds of a motte and bailey castle that is believed to date from the reign of King Stephen. During excavations in the early 1950s, a mass burial of hundreds of skeletons was unearthed here suggesting an early battle on the site, possibly the Battle of Heathfield (Hatfield) in 633 between King Edwin of Northumbria and Penda of Mercia. (See Edwinstowe – Walk 26).

If you have used the Village Hall car park, then the first port of call should be the church of St Mary. This is a wonderful building with stumpy west tower topped with battlements and corner pinnacles – otherwise the structure is plain, but long, and beautifully proportioned. In fact, it is probably the longest parish church in Nottinghamshire with an external length of 145ft. Most of what we see is of the 15th and 16th centuries but the base of the tower is 13th century. The south doorway, approached through the little 13th-century porch with Mass Dial outside, is a classic Norman one. The nave dates from the 13th century although the south wall was altered in the following two centuries. At the west end is a magnificent wooden screen which sits within an even more impressive 15th-century archway. Major restorations, supported by the 6th Duke of Portland, were carried out at the beginning of the 20th century and again in the 1930s. Unfortunately, a mass of metal joists and girders adorn the interior but these have nothing to do with restorations but rather with the threat from mining subsidence in the early 1950s and the 1980s.

The Route

1. Leave the church by the main gateway which leads from the south porch. Go right along the road, passing the Village Hall and the Cuckney Pinfold, which dates from the 18th century, then the Greendale Oak inn to your right. Go right here with the inn to your immediate right and at the cross-roads go straight over, signed to Sheffield (A616). The road passes between some fine cottages and does a gentle curve to the left then, at the sharp bend to the right, go straight on down a lesser lane with Bakers Row to your right. Where this lane bends sharply to the left, continue forward on School Lane, which ends in a parking area with the school to your right and ahead, over railings, the Cuckney Dam lake. Take the path at the top left-hand corner of the parking area to bear right *not up the house driveway*, along the waymarked path which keeps close to the railings and lake over to the right, mounting gently into woodland. A few metres on, go left up a rising path with wooden fence to your left and wooded embankment up to the right. Top the rise (known as Mill Hill) then drop down with the path as it bends right and left to a double set of stiles and steps onto the A632. Cross the road with care onto an access lane signed for Park House Farm.

2. Follow the lane for about 800m and, at the point where the hedge to the left ends, go left with a hedge to your left. Pass through a gateway (or rustic stile beside) then go right on a grassy path with hedge/bushes to your right and coniferous forest to the left. Our path continues between bushes and woodland and ignoring all side tracks, stay on a more or less straight line to a cross-track at a (false) crest. Go straight on here and follow the path as it bends to the left with a screen of trees and bushes to your right and thick woodland to the left. At the top of this slope, where the wood edge path bends sharply to the left, go straight on, leaving the trees and clipping the right-hand edge of a hedgeline to pick up a cross-field footpath. Pass a double power post to your left and continue to the hill crest where there are magnificent views to the front over Warsop in the valley below. Continue down the slope, along what is invariably an excellent path (if it should not be obvious, aim well to the

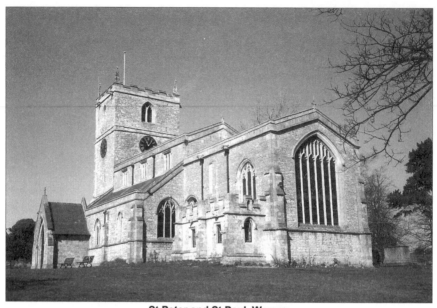

St Peter and St Paul, Warsop

left of the church tower) to pass through a hedge gap. Then, continue the line, down an embankment and over a field, through another hedge gap then forward over another field to cross a stile onto the A60. Go right along the road into the outskirts of Church Warsop, crossing over the B6031 Shirebrook road and continuing to the church.

Warsop today is a pleasant place divided in two by the River Meden. Up until the 18th century, this was forested Sherwood but then came the discovery of coal and Market Warsop swiftly developed as a mining town to the south while Warsop, with the church, grew more slowly to the north. It was not only mining though that supported this area for, long ago, it was famous for the lime which was quarried here and was in fact used in the restoration of Southwell Minster following its damage during the Civil War. In Domesday Book, the name is given as 'Wareshope' with the probable meaning 'the enclosed valley of Waer' the latter being an Old English personal name. The church of St Peter and St Paul is a magnificent building with its stubby Norman tower topped with 14th-century battlements and corner crocketed pinnacles, long slim nave, chancel, clerestory, aisles and large Early English south porch. To the south-east is a fine 16th-century add-on battlemented vestry, which is believed once to have been a chantry chapel. Inside, it is even more of a marvel with its wonderfully crude zigzag style Norman tower arch and a high rising arch into the chancel with the magnificent east window beyond. The south arcade is a fine example of Early English work, and that to the

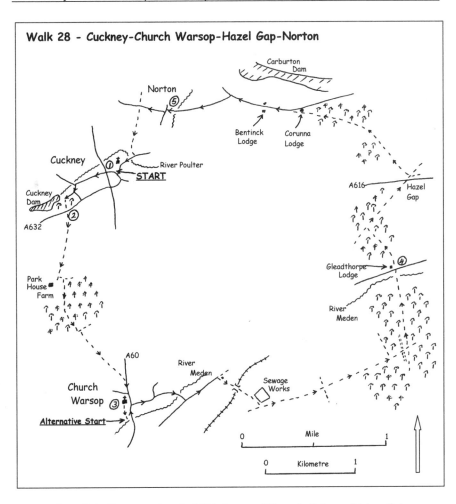

Walk 28 - Cuckney-Church Warsop-Hazel Gap-Norton

north is of the Decorated period. This is one of those buildings which well deserves a wander along the interior walls for here there are some fascinating memorials – look out for those to Samuel Hallifax who was Lord Bishop of St Asaph and Rector of Warsop, born in 1733 and died in 1790. Also for that of Sgt John Stubbins ,who lived from 1788 to 1849 and served with the 1st King's Dragoon Guards, fighting with Wellington at the Battle of Waterloo. Yet another can be found to Daniel Newton who was one of His Majesty's coroners and who died 21st May, 1764. Also, look out for the list of Rectors who are traced back to Richard de Sutton in 1245.

3. Leave the church and follow the surfaced pathway which drops down through the churchyard, bearing right to pass through a gateway into the

parking and picnic area beside the River Meden [*]. Go left onto the A60 then left again along the road pavement, passing the War Memorial to your left then go right onto Eastmans Lane, signed to Meden Vale, Welbeck Colliery and Budby. Where the road swings sharply to the left as Coggins Lane, go straight on along what is now Manor Road. Pass through a residential area and bear right with the road, soon crossing the River Meden and arriving at a T-junction. Go left along the minor road, passing farm buildings and a water pumping station to your right. At the next junction, go right onto a narrow metalled road passing a cottage to your left. Our lane rises to bridge the railway line and continues to a sewage works where we continue forward, the lane slowly deteriorating to a dirt track. Where the sewage works perimeter fence bends to the left, we arrive at a T-junction of tracks. Go left here, keeping the fence to the left and drop gently as the path meanders and slowly rises with views far over to the left of Wellbeck colliery. At a cross-track, continue forward with a hedge to your left and open field to the right and stay on this line as the path eventually drops into the corner of woodland. Keep to the main path with fine broadleaf trees to the right and hedgeline left. Ignore the finger-posted bridleway left and continue forward, now dropping through thick woodland. Ignore the wide grassy drive which crosses the front and continue for a few metres to a major cross-track with four-way finger-post with Robin Hood Way markers. Go left here, along a much deteriorated surfaced track through the trees. Emerging from the wood-land, continue to recross the River Meden and emerge onto a country road with Gleadthorpe Lodge over. (Gleadthorpe is one of a profusion of lodges built around the grounds of Welbeck Estate by the 5th Duke of Portland for his workers in the 1850s/60s. In 1875, four years before the death of the Duke, there were believed to be 35 such buildings on the estate with six more under construction! All are of Steetley Stone and all follow the same basic plan – all are beautiful little cottages).

4. Cross the road with care and continue forward through a gateway with the lodge to your left. We are soon back onto a woodland path which, after about 600m, brings us to a major finger-posted T-junction. Go right here (Robin Hood Way), on a wide earth track which continues with woodland to the left and soon, hedge to the right, to eventually emerge onto the A616 at Hazel Gap. Cross the road with care and go left (Robin Hood Way) down an earth and stone track which gently undulates, pick-ing up woodland first to one side then the other then to both sides, even-tually dropping through a shallow sandstone gorge onto another road with Corunna Lodge to the right at the junction. Go straight on along the road, (take care, this is a narrow thoroughfare with minimal verges),

soon passing Bentinck Lodge to the left and the memorial to Lord George Bentinck to the right. (This is a beautiful water trough with a carved plinth which carries an inscription to Lord George, third son of the 4th Duke of Portland who died suddenly, while walking near this spot on the 21st September, 1848. It carries a glowing tribute from Disraeli). Follow the road as it swings sharply to the left (the road ahead is private) to eventually enter the hamlet of Norton.

5. Follow the main road as it swings left at the 'green' then go right (signed to Holbeck and Worksop). The road slowly climbs out of the hamlet and 300m on, go left, (the Robin Hood Way goes off to the right) over a finger-posted stile and climb gently up a headland path with fence to your left. Continuing the line over the brow of the slope, drop down to cross a stile in the field corner then go forward to climb another stile. Then, descend a few steps onto an embankment that forms part of the old castle earthworks. Go left along the embankment with the ponds and church over to your right. Where the embankment swings to the left, drop down the slope diagonally right to a stile and over onto road. Go right up the road (there is a pavement on the far side), passing the church and so back to the start point.

29. Creswell – Whaley Thorns – Holbeck

Distance: 9½ miles (15km)

Maps: OS Landranger 120: Mansfield & Worksop, Sherwood Forest. OS Explorer 28: Sherwood Forest (to be renumbered 270)

Start: Creswell Crags Visitor Centre (GR 539744). There is ample parking at the Centre but the car park is only open between 10.30am and 5.00pm daily between February and October and on Sundays only from November to January. There are no other legal and non-inconveniencing car parking areas near the crags. If in any doubt, alternative parking may be found at one of the Poulter Country Park car parks (GR 524704 or GR 529708) (paragraph 5 below).

Churches: St Mary Magdalen, Creswell; Whaley Thorns; St Winifred, Holbeck

The Walk

A little more road and town walking than usual today but, to make up for this, some lovely woodland, fine field paths, a stupendous geological and archaeological feature and finally, a beautiful little Nottinghamshire church. Our route slips in and out of Derbyshire, visiting two of that county's places of worship and for sections of the walk we find ourselves on the Robin Hood Way and the Archaeological Way.

We start our walk at Creswell Crags which sit astride the Nottinghamshire/Derbyshire county boundary and are a site of great geological and archaeological interest. Excavations here were begun in 1874 by Sir William Boyd Dawkins and the Reverend Magens Mello and yielded a wealth of bone remains dating back to the last Ice Age, including those of mammoth, woolly rhinoceros, reindeer, hyena and cave bear. Also found have been numerous Old Stone Age artefacts, the caves and rock-shelters showing evidence of life in the later Palaeolithic period of about 10,000 years ago. Today, the magnificent limestone crags sit either side of a fine lake that was created by the Duke of Portland in the 1870s. Adjacent to the parking area is the Visitor Centre, which incorporates a small souvenir and bookshop together with snack facilities and toilets.

The Route

1. Walk eastwards along the track and away from the Visitor Centre with picnic benches to your right. Pass through a wicket gate beside metal half-gate then go left onto a finger-posted farm track (the Robin Hood Way goes forward here). At the wooden field gates across the path, go left onto a headland route with a hedge to your right, eventually emerging onto road (Henneymoor Lane). Go left along the road for about 50m and, where it swings to the left, bear right through a metal half gate and onto a path through woodland. Our route continues through the trees, eventually dropping gently to meander beside farm buildings and arrive on the A616. Go right along the road into Creswell, passing Laburnum Close to your left and at the next major junction go left onto Elmton Road, signed to the Station and Town Centre, which takes us to the church.

Creswell, situated just over the border in Derbyshire, does not appear in Domesday Book but in 1176, we have a 'Cressewella' which comes from the Old English meaning 'the spring or stream where water cress grows'. Compared with many of the towns and villages we have been exploring during our walks, Creswell is a relatively modern place, its sudden expansion due chiefly to the colliery, which was established here in 1894. The church of St Mary Magdalen is, at first sight, an ugly red brick monstrosity. It well repays a second look though. It is a long building with buttressed nave, chancel, south vestry and massive south aisle. All walls are pierced with large Perpendicular style windows with white stone surrounds and the nave is topped with a single bellcote. The east end has a nice round window and it is in this wall that the interest lies, for here can be found a stone laid on 23rd May 1899 commemorating the erection of the church by the 6th Duke if Portland. At the north-west end is the heavy tower, built of the same materials but seeming to have been an add-on – a point confirmed by a plaque informing us that it was erected by public subscription in 1927. In the graveyard are sad memorials to those killed in the Creswell Colliery disaster of 26th September, 1950.

2. Return to Elmton Road and go left. At the junction where a road goes off right to the station with, at the corner, the Colliery memorial, go left onto Welbeck Street. At the very end of the street, climb a short, steep embankment to a surfaced pathway and go right. Cross the railway line and continue to a road. Go forward along the road with industrial estate to your left and playing fields to the right and stay forward to leave the estate and join an earth and stone track. Mount the steps which lead over the embankment of the dismantled railway then descend the far side (the path starts a little to the left of the point where the steps takes us) and continue along a headland path with a hedge to your right. At the field corner, cross a stile onto a country lane.

3. Go left along the lane which rises then drops gently towards farmhouses ahead. Just before the lane swings left to pass in front of the farm, go right then left onto a dirt and stone track (we have now joined the Archaeological Way). Pass Frithwood Farm Cottage to your right then stay with this track all the way to a surfaced lane. Go right along the lane (the Archaeological Way) for 200m then left at Whaley Common, passing cottages to your right. Stay on the main lane, which drops to a T-junction in the little settlement of Whaley with The Black Horse inn to your left.

4. Go left, passing along the front of The Black Horse and, just before the converted school with its little bellcote, go right onto a finger-posted path which drops to the gateway of a large red brick cottage ahead. Go left here onto a grassy track which deteriorates as it rises through a tunnel of trees with a tinkling beck down to the left. Where a grassy track drops down to the left, bear right (with waymarker) on a path which takes us out of the trees and straight over an open field towards more woodland in the distance. At the wood edge, follow the Archaeological Way waymarker on a wide path through Scarcliffe Wood. Stay with the main drive, going straight on at two major cross-tracks. After the second of these, our path narrows slightly and bears left through, initially, broadleaf trees, then meanders on to the woodland edge. Just before the wood edge, at a junction, the Archaeological Way goes off to the right but we go left with a thick tree/hedge-line right and the woodland to the left, soon dropping quite steeply through trees onto a surfaced lane.

5. Go straight over the lane to pick up a concessionary bridleway sign-posted to Poulter Country Park which meanders upwards through trees to the edge of the parkland. Go forward over grass to a major track crossing and finger-post then go right along the track, soon passing ponds to your right. At the far end of the ponds, bear left (one of our alternative starting point car parks is to the front through a gateway here) to join a wide stony track (a blocked extension to the car park). Go left up the stony drive then right onto an earthy track with bushes and trees to your right (on the orange and white waymarked paths). Where the main track bends to the right to follow the edge of the bushes/trees, go forward onto a grassy pathway, aiming for a bench set in the hillside ahead where we rejoin the main track. Go forward along the track (orange and white waymarkers still), rising gently to the brow where there are fine views ahead. Follow the main path (white waymarker now – the orange route has gone off to the left) which drops gently to bear right over a railway

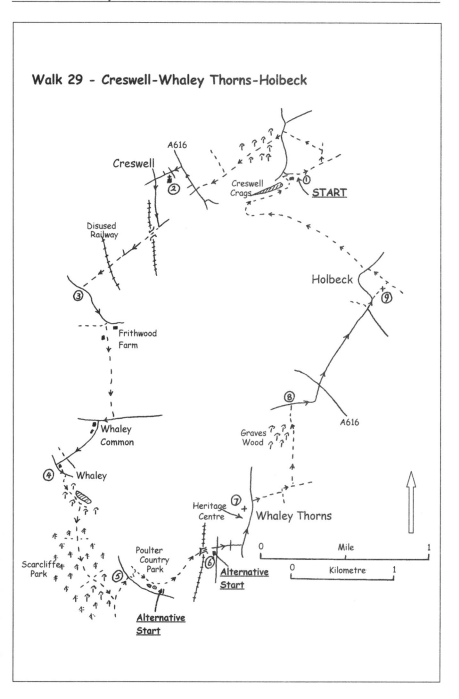

Walk 29 - Creswell-Whaley Thorns-Holbeck

bridge to continue beside the park car park, which is another alternative start point for this walk.

6. Pass out of the car park to the junction of North Street and Bathurst Terrace with, across the junction to the left a coal truck with the inscription 'Langwith Colliery, 1876-1978'. Go straight over the junction and drop down the road (Main Street). At the T-junction, go left, signed to the Heritage Centre and at the end of the terraces, to the left, is the Heritage Centre itself, which is well worth a visit. Our route continues down the main road, passing the Community Centre and so to the gateway which leads to the church.

Once a thriving mining community, reminders of the great Langwith Colliery are not easy to find today. But the little colliery truck we passed close to the car park gives a hint and the Heritage Centre is an excellent source of information. The real gem though is the magnificent Poulter Country Park over which we have recently walked and which was once a mass of spoil heaps. It is wonderful to know that the area is at last being regenerated and supplied with such magnificent recreational facilities. The church at Whaley Thorns is a strange modern building with a lovely approach along a tree-lined avenue. Sadly neglected, with its plain windows covered with mesh, it is though, a most unusual structure with plain ashlar nave and chancel and an odd-looking tower topped by a steep-sided Chinese pagoda-looking red-tiled roof. Thus, although really outside the scope of this book, it well repays a short visit if only for its peculiarity.

7. Return to the road and go left, passing Woodland View then the school to your left and just beyond, cross the road to go right through a kissing gate and onto a finger-posted footpath which takes us back into Nottinghamshire. Follow the headland with a hedge to your right and, at the field corner, cross the stile beside field gate to go left with stone wall to your left then right, with hedge and wall to your left. At the point where the first hedgeline can be seen coming in from the left, go left, over steps in the wall, onto a gently rising headland path with hedge to the right and woodland ahead. At the field corner, go straight on into the trees (Graves Wood) and follow a path with thick woodland to your left and hedge/trees to the right. Emerging from the trees, continue forward for about 20m with a hedge to your right then where this hedge swings off to the right, bear gently left, over the field to arrive on a minor road.

8. Go right along the road, dropping gently and follow it as it swings left to join the relatively busy A616. Go straight over and mount the gentle slope, which flattens and brings us into the little village of Holbeck. Pass the road signed to Norton and Cuckney and go straight on, signed to Worksop. The road swings sharply to the left to enter the 30mph speed

limit and here, go forward through a wooden lych gate in the hedge and follow a ridge path between wooden fences to drop to the high hedge surrounding the church. Go to the right with the hedge to your left and follow the path that bends through an overgrown archway (with sliding wooden bars) and out into the churchyard of St Winifred.

St Winifred, Holbeck

Holbeck does not appear in Domesday Book but comes as 'Holebek' in 1180, the name deriving from the Old Scandinavian meaning 'the stream in a hollow'. It is a tiny estate village, famous as the place where the 6th Duke of Portland raised his race horses but it is the wonderful little church that really attracts us today. This was built in 1915 by the 6th Duke and dedicated in the name of his wife – Winifred, whose tomb can be seen in the churchyard. It is a very simple and very attractive little building in a mock Norman style. There is a single bellcote and north-west porch, combined nave and chancel with low apsidal east end. We have approached the church from the south, but the main entrance, to the north, is guarded by a massive stone lych gate, also in the Norman style. The wonders of this church, though, are its monuments, which can be seen within the enclosure at the east end of the building and along the base of a massive cross marked in the grass at the west end. These provide a fascinating family tree of the Duke's of Portland through the recent past and include Winifred, Duchess of Portland (1864-1954) and her husband the 6th Duke of Portland (1857-1943). Buried here also are Lt Col Lord Charles Cavendish Bentinck (1868-1956) and Lord William Augustus Cavendish Bentinck. Ivy, Duchess of Portland and her husband the 7th Duke (1893-1977) and Victoria Margaret, daughter of the 7th Duke and wife of Prince Gaetano Parente (1918-1955). What an amazing find in such a lovely lonely spot!

9. Leave the church though the mock Norman lych gate that leads onto a lane and go left along the lovely tree-lined avenue to emerge beside gateway onto a country lane. Go left, passing the telephone box, then right onto a finger-posted (Robin Hood Way) driveway with cottage on your right. Where the driveway swings into the cottage grounds, go straight on, rising between thick hedges and emerge into a field corner. Go forward along a headland path with fence and hedge to your left. Cross the stile in the field corner and continue forward, still with hedge to your left, dropping gently to cross another stile and continue on a path between two sections of field. At the far side of the field, cross the stile and continue the line along what is now a headland path with thick hedge/trees to your right. Pass an overgrown stile to your right (an old field corner) and at the next (real) field corner, cross the stile and bear slightly to the right, gently up-slope, keeping parallel to the hedge to your right and aiming for a thick hedgeline and trees ahead. Soon we join the wood edge and follow it upward with the bushes/trees to the right. Before long we are walking parallel to a stone wall to our right then cross a stile in a wooden fence and continue to a magnificent viewpoint over Creswell. (The little building down to the front is a Victorian pump house). A clear path takes us round to the right to drop quite steeply over embedded boulders to a cross-track. Go right here, still descending, to a stone stile then on, bearing right through a bridlegate and into the Creswell Crags Valley. Follow the main path with the towering cliffs to your right and stream then lake to the left. At the end of the lake go left, (into Derbyshire) leaving the cliffs behind and with lake to the left, pass through a gateway. Go right, (before the road) onto a pathway, which drops with the beck down to your right then slowly mounts between trees to arrive at the Visitor Centre access lane. Go right and so back to the start point.

30. Worksop – Welbeck – Belph – Darfoulds

Distance: 11 miles (17.5km)

Maps: OS Landranger 120: Mansfield & Worksop, Sherwood Forest. OS Explorer 28: Sherwood Forest (to be renumbered 270)

Start: Worksop Castle (GR 583788). There is 'pay and display' parking close to the castle but a better parking area (also 'pay and display') is on Central Avenue adjacent to Pickwicks (restaurant and pub). The car park is signed from Newcastle Avenue and coming from the by-pass, is approached via Stubbing Lane. If using this facility, the castle is reached as follows: Return to Central Avenue and go right, walking away from Pickwicks. Take the first right (King Street) and at the junction with Newcastle Road, go right, crossing as quickly as possible then left up Norfolk Street (immediately before the garage). The castle mound is up to the left.

Churches: St Anne, Worksop

The Walk

We complete the circle of our walks today with another Worksop beginning and, although to describe it as a 'church walk' might be stretching the imagination just a little bit, it does take in a church, and a castle and even an abbey (from a distance), but the joy here is the walk itself. It is a little longer than normal but it has a bit of everything – cross-field footpaths, green lanes, beautiful woodland, a little waterside-walking, some fine historical monuments and a hidden hamlet. Most of the walk is within Nottinghamshire but we do stray briefly into Derbyshire.

Worksop itself was described in Walk 1 but its castle is not well publicised and although little more than a large grassy mound, the short climb to the top is well worth the effort for from here there are fine views over the town. The earliest habitation of the site can be traced back to Neolithic times but the earliest recorded occupation comes from Domesday Book which described the land as belonging to the Saxon Lord Elsi. Following the Norman occupation it passed to Roger de Busli (of Bully) then in the 12th century, to the de Lovetot family then the de Furnivals and, in the late 14th century, John Talbot, 1st Earl of Shrewsbury had ownership. In 1839 it was sold to the Dukes of Newcastle and in 1988 was purchased by the Bassetlaw District Council and developed into the lovely viewpoint it is today.

The Route

1. Return to Newcastle Avenue and go left along the road for about 500m, the tower of St Anne's church soon appearing ahead. Immediately beyond the church, go left into Water Meadows (road) to find the main entrance to the church grounds.

The massive bulk of the church of St Anne occupies a dominant position on the corner of Newcastle Avenue and Water Meadows with the fine war memorial cross on the grass triangle to its front. It is a fairly modern building constructed in the Perpendicular style in 1911-1912. The main structure is a combined

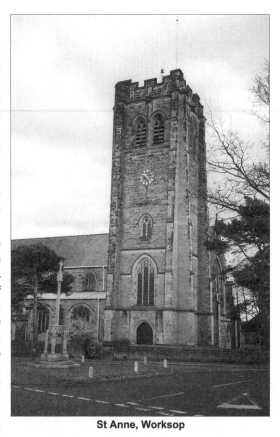

St Anne, Worksop

nave and chancel with side vestry-like protrusions and a magnificent bulky tower which appears to have been added to the north-west corner of the main building as an after-thought. From the outside, this does not look the most pleasing of churches but inside there is a wonderful feeling of height and simplicity with lovely octagonal aisle columns and a magnificent east window. Also inside is an attractive octagonal carved font and a fine tomb with the recumbent form of Sir John Robinson of Worksop Manor, the builder and founder of the church who died in 1929. There is also a list if vicars going back to 1913!

2. Back on Water Meadows, go left, following the road through a residential housing area. Pass Saxton Close, Devonshire Street, Laburnum Close, Poplar Close and Robinson Drive to your left then, a little over 100m on, cross the road to go right onto a wide finger-posted track between garden fences (house No 80 is to your right). At the end of the fence to the right, leave the main track and go right, with the waymarker, then left with hedges to your left and wire fence to the right. Follow the path as it bends to the left between wooden fences and continue to steps on your right. Mount these then descend to the busy A57 trunk road. *Take the greatest of care crossing this hectic thoroughfare* and having safely reached the far side, climb the steps then drop down to cross two stiles into a field corner. Follow the headland path with hedgeline to your left and, over to the right amongst the trees, occasional glimpses of all that remains of Worksop Manor. (Today's Manor comprises of little more than the converted servant's quarters and an Elizabethan hunting lodge. The first mention of a major building on the site is in the 15th century when the occupant was John Talbot, 1st Earl of Shrewsbury. Towards the end of the 16th century, the 6th Earl, who was the fourth and last husband of Bess of Hardwick, rebuilt the house as a magnificent mansion, which seems to have been a cross between Longleat and Hardwick. It was the 6th Earl who was responsible for the custody of Mary Queen of Scots and she was kept here in 1583. Through marriage, the house eventually fell to the Dukes of Norfolk, the 9th Duke planning a rebuild which would have made it 'the greatest and grandest private house in England' but following his death in 1767, the plans were shelved, his successors being more interested in restoring their castle at Arundel in Sussex. The estate was sold to the 4th Duke of Newcastle in 1839 but he was much more interested in his home at Clumber and virtually demolished the Worksop property, finally selling it off in 1890). Our route stays with the headland for almost three-quarters of a mile before crossing a rustic stile onto a stony lane. Bear left (forward) along the lane, walking gently up-slope and at a cross-track continue forward, eventually passing through a gateway and into woodland. Stay with the main track through the trees for about half a mile when it drops to a clearing around South Lodge. Just before the lodge fence, leave the main track which swings to the left and bear gently right along a grassy path with a hedge to your right and garden fence/lodge left, passing through a wicket gate and onto a major track. Opposite is a fascinating little piece of eccentric history, the entrance to one of the 5th Duke of Portland's tunnels.

South Lodge marks the southern extent of the Worksop Manor estate. Onwards is the splendid estate of Welbeck, whose abbey is one of the largest and most splendid houses in England. It is the seat of the Cavendish-Bentinck family although large parts of the building have been in use as a military college since shortly after the Second World War. The abbey was founded as a Premonstratensian house in 1153 but after the Dissolution it passed through various hands until in 1597, Sir Charles Cavendish (the third son of Bess of Hardwick) leased it from his brother-in-law and ten years later, purchased it.

Through a complicated line, the property eventually passed to William Bentink, 2ⁿᵈ Duke of Portland since when the succession has been direct. The 3ʳᵈ Duke was twice Prime Minister under George III and the 5ᵗʰ Duke, who succeeded to the title in 1854 was an eccentric. He was thwarted in love by the Covent Garden opera singer Adelaide Kemble and never married. Although he later became MP for King's Lynn, he slowly developed into a recluse, hiding himself away in just four or five rooms of the huge house while spending colossal sums on building work above and, especially, below ground. Underground he had constructed for him a vast ballroom, the largest unsupported room in Europe and around this were a number of other rooms, including a suite of libraries and a vast bachelor's hall. Subterranean passages were fitted with tramlines so that food could be carried in trucks from the kitchen. Outside the house, he built tunnels to Worksop and to the new riding school and stables that he built in the park. The hollows that we shall pass on our onward route mark the location of skylights, which were alternated with gas-lights to ensure the safety of passengers on the road below. He died in 1879 and his successor, the 6ᵗʰ Duke, considered abandoning the house because of the awful state in which it had been left. Fortunately, he instituted a major reconstruction and by 1881 sufficient progress had been made for him to invite the Prince of Wales to a great party there. A fire in 1902 spurred on further refurbishment and the result is the wonderful building that exists today.

3. Go left along the track for a few metres then right, as directed by the finger-post, with the tunnel entrance complex to your right. At a fence, go right again (now picking up the Robin Hood Way) through the waymarked bridle gate and continue with a wooden fence to your left. 30m on, go left through another bridle gate and continue forward on a track between open fields. To the right and hidden amongst the field growth can be found the skylights of the underground tunnel constructed by the 5ᵗʰ Duke – now capped while, in the distance to the front left, we get our first glimpses of Welbeck Abbey. Our route crosses a narrow neck of land over the Abbey's Great Lake and at a T-junction, go right. At the next junction, go right again onto a surfaced lane and where this bends to the right, go left onto a finger-posted grassy track with thick hedges and trees to your left. Follow the path as it bends to the right with a wooden fence left and the college playing fields over. At the end of the playing fields, continue forward with bushes and trees to your left and wooden fence to the right. At a T-junction with a stony/concrete track, go right with, over to your left, the Riding School constructed by the eccentric 5ᵗʰ Duke. Stay with the main lane as it drops to pass Oakstetts Lodge then becomes a beautiful tree-lined driveway that leads to the busy A60.

4. The Robin Hood Way goes forward here to Creswell Crags but our route is to the right along the road (there is a pavement on the far side but take

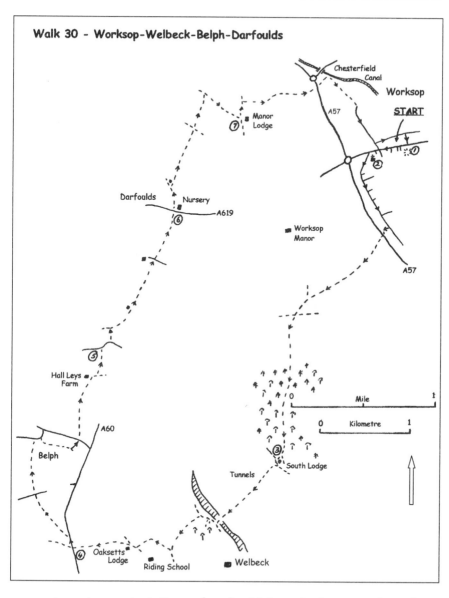

Walk 30 - Worksop-Welbeck-Belph-Darfoulds

great care in crossing). Cross a brook which marks the county boundary with Derbyshire then bear left onto a finger-posted green lane, passing beside a small patch of woodland (Ladycroft Wood) to arrive at a minor road. Cross with care and continue over a stile at the far side to pick up a stony track which runs forward over a mini lunar landscape of spoil heaps. Soon we cross a culvert then walk parallel to a (dangerous) lake down to our right, our path rising gently with embankments up to the left. At the top of the slope, continue forward with the houses of Hodthorpe in the distance ahead and the hamlet of Belph down to the front right then drop gently over grass to a stile over onto a narrow road. Go right along the road, passing a couple of stone cottages and where the road bends to the left, go right down a finger-posted path beside telephone and post boxes. Our path leads us to a babbling brook, which we follow to our left into the hamlet of Belph. Go forward between the cottages then take the first lane to the left, again between cottages, and so to a road crossing. Go straight over the road to pass through a hedge gap and cross a plank bridge onto field edge. (The path onwards from this point is usually well defined but in case of difficulty, the rough aiming point over the next three fields should be Hall Leys Farm that can be seen in the distance). Cross the first field and pass through the stiled hedge gap and continue to the next gap (now aiming slightly to the left of the farm). In the third field, aim slightly to the right of the farm buildings, eventually joining a surfaced access track with the farm buildings to your left. Go to the right then left along the track to arrive on road.

5. Go right along the road, passing sewage works to your left and where the road bends sharply to the right, go left onto a finger-posted bridleway (Ratcliffe Lane) which ascends as a stony track. At the top of the slope, ignore the waymarked footpath to the left and go right between cottages on the main lane. The lane swings to the left and we stay on this route now for almost a mile to arrive on the busy A619.

6. Cross the road with care and continue along a finger-posted track with the Darfoulds Nursery to the right. Our track climbs gently and we follow it as it bends to the left then, immediately before the cottage to your right, go right over a stile beside metal field gate with the cottage over hedge to the left. We follow a headland path with a hedge to our right as it drops gently with views of Worksop far over to the right. At the bottom of the incline, ignore side tracks and *continue forward*, still along the headland with a hedge to the right and with a view, over to the right, of the magnificent Manor Lodge. Eventually, at the far field corner, cross a stile onto a stony track and go right with, initially, hedges/trees to the left to arrive on a lane with the lodge over.

7. Go left along the lane to pass through a metal field gate and onto a stony track between hedges. About 100m on, cross a beck and immediately go right, down steps and pick up a path which meanders through trees with the stream to your right. Cross a footbridge and continue through wood-

land, eventually crossing two more bridges and swinging left to emerge at a field corner. Continue forward along the headland with hedge/trees to your left and soon, an industrial estate over. Pass beneath power cables and continue to a hedge gap at the field corner to climb steps to the busy A57 trunk road. Cross the road with care (there is a central reservation), and pick up a finger-posted path which leads down steps to cross a stile into field. Bear left over the field, aiming for the right-hand of the two huge chimneys in the distance and arrive on a surfaced lane with the Chesterfield Canal ahead. Go right along the lane (Stubbing Lane), soon crossing the river Ryton, continuing past the Worksop Rugby Club and into the outskirts of Worksop itself. Follow the road all the way to the junction with Central Avenue and go left to pass Pickwicks and so back to the start point of our final church walk in north Nottinghamshire.

Glossary

Although every effort has been made to avoid any technical vocabulary, a few explanations might be of value.

Apse
The polygonal or semicircular end to the chancel. Such chancels can be described as Apsidal. Examples can be found at Besthorpe and Shireoaks.

Arcade
The series of columns or pillars supporting arches which can be found separating the nave from the aisles.

Ashlar
Large squared blocks of dressed stone used to surface exterior walls of coarser masonry.

Bellcote
A small tower or arch that contains a bell or bells usually sited on the roof at the west end of the church. Examples are to be found at Besthorpe, Carburton, Cottam, Girton (where it is centrally placed), Moorhouse, Ranskill, Stokeham and Thorney.

Chancel
The eastern continuation of the nave which contains the altar.

Clerestory
An extension upwards of the nave walls above the aisles. The insertion of windows permitted more light into the church.

Corbel
A block of stone which projects from a wall to support a beam or arch.

Crockets
Projecting buds placed along the sloping sides of a structure. Commonly found on the spires and pinnacles of our Perpendicular churches.

Cruciform
A church plan in the shape of a cross.

Hatchment
Coat of arms or family crest, often diamond-shaped, found on the interior walls of many of our churches.

Nave
Main body of the church set to the west of the chancel.

Spires
Our area is not noted for its spires but we do visit four churches with broach spires – at Boughton, Edwinstowe, Harby and Misterton, seven of the recessed type (Clumber, Grove, Scrooby, South Anston, Tuxford, West Retford and Weston on Trent) plus a tiny spirelet at Eaton.

Tracery
Ornamental stonework in a window or screen.

Transept
An arm of the crossing in a cruciform church.

Transom
Horizontal cross-bar which spans a window or the top of a door. There is a fine example of the window type at Edwinstowe.

Triforium
A gallery or wall passage between the top of the main arcade and the clerestory above as seen in Worksop Priory church.

Tympanum
Space between the lintel at the top of a doorway and the arch shape above it. There is a magnificent example at Everton.

Index

(References are to Walk numbers, not page numbers)

Also of Interest:

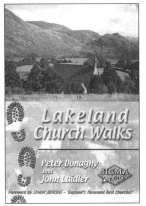

LAKELAND CHURCH WALKS
Peter Donaghy and John Laidler
Foreword by Simon Jenkins – author of "England's 1000 Best Churches". This is the first walking guide based on Lakeland churches. A superb selection of over 50 churches open to visitors, with many photographs. Trace the impact of famous people, patrons and personalities such as Wordsworth, Ruskin, the Dacres, Lady Anne Clifford, the Beauty of Buttermere and even Tarzan! £8.95

NORTHUMBRIA CHURCH WALKS
Peter Donaghy and John Laidler
Foreword by Sting – international rock star and conservationist. Hills, dales and magnificent coastlines are combined with a selection of over 40 churches open to visitors, with many photographs. Insight is provided into our cultural and artistic heritage with fine examples of stained glass windows, ancient crosses, medieval fonts, wood carvings and sculptures old and new. £8.95

WEST SUSSEX CHURCH WALKS
Diana Pé
"The inspiration for this book sprung from a delight in wandering the downs and seeing in the distance an unpretentious church whose tower rises above a quiet hamlet." says Diana Pe. Her carefully planned walks range from 3 to 10 miles and cover a variety of terrain from coastal plains and woodland to riversides and gently undulating hills. Fully illustrated with sketch maps and photographs. £7.95

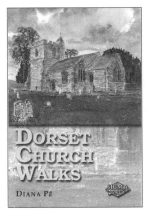

DORSET CHURCH WALKS
Diana Pé
Take a glimpse into the past - the absorbing history of each church reveals much about the lives of those who lived there in the past. Enjoy a tremendous diversity of walking opportunities: from exhilarating routes by the spectacularly beautiful Dorset coast to peaceful walks around the golden town of Sherborne and in the Vale of Blackmore. Explore Dorset's exceptional literary heritage at sites associated with Thomas Hardy and William Barnes and many others. £7.95

All of our books are available through booksellers. In case of difficulty, or for a free catalogue, please contact: **SIGMA LEISURE, 1 SOUTH OAK LANE, WILMSLOW, CHESHIRE SK9 6AR.**
Phone: 01625-531035 Fax: 01625-536800. E-mail: info@sigmapress.co.uk
Web site: http//www.sigmapress.co.uk
MASTERCARD and VISA orders welcome.

The Churches Conservation Trust

The Churches Conservation Trust cares for 325 churches of outstanding historic, architectural or archaeological importance.

- The Trust warmly welcomes visitors throughout the year to its churches which are scattered throughout England

- The Trust was set up in 1969 to preserve and repair churches which are no longer needed for regular worship

- Many of our churches are hidden gems, beautifully set and ideal for discovering on a walk, cycle ride or day out; others can be found in market towns or bustling cities

- All our churches have something special to offer – breathtaking architecture, brilliant stained glass, fascinating monuments, ancient wallpaintings…..

- All are either opened regularly or have keyholders nearby

For more information on Trust churches and opening arrangements visit our website at **www.visitchurches.org.uk**

Alternatively, **write to us** at 89 Fleet Street, London EC4Y 1DH for a free copy of Your Starter for 50 booklet and County leaflets (please specify county/ies required).

www.visitchurches.org.uk

Registered Charity No. 258612